THE STATELY HOUSES, PALACES & CASTLES OF
GEORGIAN, VICTORIAN & MODERN BRITAIN

FROM GEORGE I TO ELIZABETH II, 1714 O THE PRESENT DAY

THE STATELY HOUSES, PALACES & CASTLES OF
GEORGIAN, VICTORIAN & MODERN BRITAIN

FROM GEORGE I TO ELIZABETH II, 1714 TO THE PRESENT DAY

CHARLES PHILLIPS

CONSULTANT: PROFESSOR RICHARD G WILSON FRHistS

southwater

This edition is published
by Southwater
an imprint of Anness Publishing Ltd
Hermes House
88–89 Blackfriars Road
London SE1 8HA
tel. 020 7401 2077
fax 020 7633 9499

www.southwaterbooks.com;
www.annesspublishing.com

Anness Publishing has a new picture
agency outlet for images for publishing,
promotions or advertising. Please visit
our website www.practicalpictures.com
for more information.

UK distributor: Book Trade Services
tel. 0116 2759086; fax 0116 2759090;
uksales@booktradeservices.com;
exportsales@booktradeservices.com

North American distributor: National
Book Network; tel. 301 459 3366
fax 301 429 5746; www.nbnbooks.com

Australian distributor: Pan Macmillan
Australia; tel. 1300 135 113; fax 1300 135
103; customer.service@macmillan.com.au

New Zealand distributor: David Bateman
Ltd; tel. (09) 415 7664; fax (09) 415 8892

Publisher: Joanna Lorenz
Editor: Joy Wotton
Designer: Nigel Partridge

Illustrators: Anthony Duke, Rob Highton
and Vanessa Card
Proofreading Manager: Lindsay Zamponi

At Anness Publishing we believe that
business should be conducted in an ethical
and ecologically sustainable way, with
respect for the environment and a proper
regard to the replacement of the natural
resources we employ.

As a publisher, we use a lot of wood pulp
in high-quality paper for printing, and
that wood commonly comes from spruce
trees. We are therefore currently growing
more than 750,000 trees in three Scottish
forest plantations: Berrymoss (130 hectares
/320 acres), West Touxhill (125 hectares/
305 acres) and Deveron Forest (75 hectares/
185 acres). The forests we manage contain
more than 3.5 times the number of trees
employed each year in making paper for
the books we manufacture.

Because of this ongoing ecological
investment programme, you, as our
customer, can have the pleasure and
reassurance of knowing that a tree is being
cultivated on your behalf to naturally
replace the materials used to make the
book you are holding.

Our forestry programme is run in
accordance with the UK Woodland
Assurance Scheme (UKWAS) and will be
certified by the internationally recognized
Forest Stewardship Council (FSC). The

FSC is a non-government organization
dedicated to promoting responsible
management of the world's forests.
Certification ensures forests are managed
in an environmentally sustainable and
socially responsible way. For further
information about this scheme, go to
www.annesspublishing.com/trees

Previously published as part of a larger volume,
*The Complete Illustrated Guide to the Castles,
Palaces & Stately Houses of Britain and Ireland*

PUBLISHER'S NOTE
Although the advice and information in
this book are believed to be accurate and
true at the time of going to press, neither
the authors nor the publisher can accept
any legal responsiblity or liability for any
errors or omissions that may be made.

Page 1: Stourhead.
Page 2: Buckingham Palace.
Page 3: Castle Howard.
Page 4 left to right: Blenheim Palace,
Kew Palace and Windsor Castle.
Page 5 left to right: Arundel Castle,
Balmoral and Eilean Donan Castle.

CONTENTS

INTRODUCTION

For around 500 years from the Tudor age to the early 20th century, aristocratic houses served as magnets for the greatest artists and sculptors of the age. Castle Howard, Holkham Hall, Stowe House, Alnwick Castle, Castell Coch and other great Georgian, Regency and Victorian houses embodied and contained the work of creative geniuses among architects, designers, painters, sculptors and garden planners. These grand ancestral seats were doubtless what novelist Evelyn Waugh had in mind when in 1959 he called the country house Britain's 'chief national artistic achievement'. For many years, royal palaces were overshadowed by the grand country homes of the British aristocracy, but in the 1800s at Windsor Castle and the Brighton Pavilion, at Osborne, Balmoral and Buckingham Palace, Britain's monarchs brought royal buildings near to the forefront of contemporary architecture.

Left: Buckingham Palace. The Duke of Buckingham's town house became a royal residence in 1762 and was transformed into a palace by John Nash after 1826. Its east front was remodelled by Sir Aston Webb in 1913.

GEORGIAN, VICTORIAN
AND MODERN COUNTRY HOUSES

 The first decades that followed the accession of the Hanoverian dynasty in 1714 represent the nadir of royal building in England. When in London, George I and George II made do with the modest Kensington Palace, created by William III, and the increasingly shabby St James's Palace, built by Henry VIII. Neither king liked England much and their affections really lay with the palace of Herrenhausen in Hanover.

For much of the 18th century, indeed, many Englishmen were rather uncomfortably aware that the monarchy lacked a grand palace in the capital. St James's was considered inadequate: the novelist and journalist Daniel Defoe dismissed it as 'really mean' in comparison to the glories of the royal court it housed. He also added that, while the English court was more magnificent than any other in Europe. 'this palace comes beneath those of the most petty princes'.

Below: The Prince Regent and John Nash used an Islamic-influenced 'Hindoo' style for the Brighton Pavilion, begun in 1815.

LATE GEORGIAN CHANGES

In his 60-year reign (1760-1820), George III undertook improvements at Windsor Castle. He also bought Kew Palace and – as a family retreat from court life at St James's – Buckingham House, which later became the kind of grand metropolitan palace that might have pleased Defoe. But it was only with George IV that royal building really began again. With Jeffry Wyatville, George was largely responsible for transforming Windsor Castle into the picturesque 'Gothic' residence that wins the admiration of visitors from all over the world; with John Nash, Henry Holland, Thomas Hopper and James Wyatt, he created the extravagant Carlton House in central London (demolished in 1827); and, again with Nash, he built the exotic Royal Pavilion in Brighton and began the transformation of Buckingham House into a great palace.

VICTORIA'S CONTRIBUTION

In Queen Victoria's reign, Buckingham Palace was named the monarch's official London residence and given the east front that is now its celebrated 'public

Above: Robert Adam transformed the 16th-century Osterley House, Middlesex, by adding a 'neoclassical' facade in c.1763.

face'. With her husband, Prince Albert, she built two substantial family retreats far removed from her public life in London: Osborne House on the Isle of Wight and Balmoral Castle in the Grampian region of Scotland. Balmoral Castle has remained popular with the royal family and together with Sandringham House in Norfolk – acquired by Edward VII in 1862 while still Prince of Wales – is Elizabeth II's principal retreat from royal life at Buckingham Palace, Windsor Castle and Holyroodhouse in Edinburgh.

BRITISH COUNTRY HOUSES

In the 18th century, when Britain's kings occupied the rundown St James's Palace and the uninspiring Kensington Palace, the country's powerful Whig aristocrats lived and entertained in extravagant style in country houses such as Castle Howard in Yorkshire, Stowe House in Buckinghamshire and Chatsworth in Derbyshire. With buildings designed by architects of genius, such as John Vanbrugh, William Kent, Nicholas Hawksmoor and Colen Campbell, standing in gardens and parklands designed by Charles Bridgeman, Kent and 'Capability' Brown, 18th-century aristocrats may well have enjoyed the period of highest achievement in the history of the British country house.

In the 19th century, the wealth generated by Victorian Britain's empire and industry funded another great age of country house building. Architects such as Anthony Salvin and William Burges romantically renovated some great castles such as Alnwick, Muncaster, Cardiff and Castell Coch.

DECLINE AND FALL

In the 20th century, however, although fine new houses such as Castle Drogo and Manderston were built, the general picture for country houses was bleak. Following agricultural depression and social changes, partly resulting from wider democratization, heavy taxation and punitive death duties, many owners struggled to survive. Houses fell into ruin, and were demolished or sold for institutional use, while treasured collections of paintings, sculpture and books were sold to overseas buyers.

SAVED FOR THE NATION

Some estate owners showed great ingenuity in making their houses pay: in the 1960s, the 6th Marquess of Bath, introduced lions to his estate at Longleat

Below: Robert Adam evoked the grandeur of ancient Rome in his lavish decoration of the Ante-room at Syon House, Middlesex.

in Wiltshire to help attract paying visitors in order to fund the house; at Loseley Park in Surrey, James More-Molyneux established a thriving dairy business. Many houses were saved by the Country House scheme of 1937, under which owners unable to meet death duties could pass the property to the National Trust, an independent charity founded in 1895, and later government schemes under which restoration and maintenance grants were made and tax concessions granted in return for house owners opening their doors to the public for an agreed number of days each year.

Above: Belvoir Castle, Leicestershire, is one of many castles rebuilt in the 'Gothic Revival' style in the 19th century.

House after house passed from private hands to the National Trust and English Heritage (a government organization charged with caring for England's historic environment) or their equivalents in Scotland, Wales and Ireland.

The country house was for many centuries a central point in local life: its owner was supported by and supportive of the locality. In the 19th and early 20th centuries, these houses briefly became little more than a locus of privilege, a treasured private possession. Since the end of World War II, however, they have become part of a shared and treasured national heritage – an embodiment, like the ruined castles that also dot the countryside, and the palaces and other royal residences, of the glories and storied achievements of Britain's past.

USING THIS BOOK
Many of the houses described in this book changed over time as architects added new buildings to the original design or modernized old structures. Therefore, some great historic houses appear in several sections of the book.

ENGLAND TIMELINE

Above: Blenheim Palace is one of Sir John Vanbrugh's masterpieces.

Above: George IV and Wyatville rebuilt Windsor Castle in Gothic Revival style.

Above: Castle Drogo, Devon, Lutyens' extraordinary 20th-century castle.

1714–99

1715 Colen Campbell begins Wanstead House in Essex.

*c.*1720 Castle Howard close to completion.

1722 Blenheim Palace nears completion.

1722 James Gibbs builds Ditchley Park.

1723 Campbell completes Mereworth Castle, Kent, based on a villa by Palladio.

1725 The 3rd Earl of Burlington builds Chiswick House (now in west London).

1734 William Kent begins building Holkham Hall, Norfolk.

1734 Kent builds the south portico, Stowe House, Buckinghamshire.

1747 Horace Walpole begins rebuilding his villa at Strawberry Hill, Middlesex.

1751–57 'Capability' Brown landscapes the park at Petworth House, Sussex.

1758 Robert Adam begins work at Kedleston Hall, Derbyshire.

1762 Robert Adam begins work on the interior of Syon House, Middlesex.

1762 George III buys the future Buckingham Palace as a family house.

1764–79 Robert Adam rebuilds Kenwood House in Hampstead.

1770s Sir William Chambers extends Marlborough House to three storeys.

1781 George III buys the Dutch House in Kew, south-west London.

1783 The Prince of Wales begins refurbishment of Carlton House, London.

1788 James Wyatt completes work on Heveningham Hall, Suffolk.

1800–1899

1803 John Nash builds Cronkhill in Shropshire.

1805 Sandridge Park built in Devon, another Nash house.

1806–14 North front of Longleat House, Wiltshire, rebuilt by Jeffry Wyatt.

1810–20 Robert Smirke builds Eastnor Castle in the Norman Revival style.

1815–23 John Nash builds the Royal Pavilion, Brighton.

1823 onwards George IV and Jeffry Wyatville rebuild Windsor Castle in the Gothic Revival style.

1826 George IV begins the conversion of Buckingham House into a palace.

1837–45 Anthony Salvin builds Harlaxton Hall in Lincolnshire.

1845–51 Prince Albert builds Osborne House, Isle of Wight.

1847–50 An east front is added to Buckingham Palace.

*c.*1850 Anthony Salvin rebuilds Alnwick Castle, Northumberland.

1855 Paxton begins building Mentmore Towers, Buckinghamshire, for Baron Mayer Amschel de Rothschild.

1862 The future Edward VII buys the Sandringham estate in Norfolk.

1873–76 Pugin rebuilds Carlton Towers, Yorkshire, in the Victorian Gothic style.

1870 Buckler begins lavish rebuilding of Arundel Castle, West Sussex.

1874–79 Destailleur builds Waddesdon Manor, Buckinghamshire.

1900–TODAY

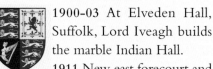

1900–03 At Elveden Hall, Suffolk, Lord Iveagh builds the marble Indian Hall.

1911 New east forecourt and Victoria Memorial at Buckingham Palace.

1912–30 Edwin Lutyens builds Castle Drogo, Devon, for Julius Charles Drewe.

1913 East front of Buckingham Palace refaced in Portland stone by Aston Webb.

1931–36 Courtaulds restore the 15th-century Great Hall at Eltham Palace, and build a superb Art Deco house.

1958–62 Phillimore builds Arundel Park for the Duke and Duchess of Norfolk.

1961–62 Patrick Gwynne builds an ultramodern country house at Witley Park, Surrey.

1963–65 The unusual country house of Stratton Park, Hampshire, incorporates the surviving Doric portico of a ruined 'Greek Revival' house.

1967–71 Raymond Erith and Quinlan Terry build Kings Walden Bury, Herts.

1971–73 John Dennys designs Eaton Hall, Cheshire, in the Modern style. In 1989 the house is refaced in a more traditional guise.

1976 Elizabeth II buys Gatcombe Park, Gloucestershire, for Princess Anne and Captain Mark Phillips.

1980 Duchy of Cornwall buys Highgrove in Gloucestershire, for Prince Charles.

2003 Quinlan Terry's Ferne Park, Dorset, wins acclaim.

N
W **E**
S

SCOTLAND

Banburgh Castle

Alnwick Castle

Seaton Delaval Hall

North Sea

Muncaster Castle

Castle Howard

Harewood House

Irish Sea

Brodsworth Hall

Heaton Hall

ENGLAND

Chatsworth

The Wash

Kedleston Hall

Nottingham Castle

Holkham Hall

Blickling

Sandringham

Houghton Hall

Rousham House

Weston Park

Arbury Hall

Elveden Hall

Upton House

Stoke Park Pavilions

Althorp

Woburn Abbey

Eastnor Castle

Ditchley Park

Stowe House

Hellens

Sudeley Castle

Waddesdon Manor

Knebworth House

WALES

Blenheim Palace

Hughenden Manor

Cliveden

Eltham Palace

Windsor Castle

Bristol Channel

Prior Park

Highclere Castle

Polesden Lacy

Port Lympne

Stourhead

Petworth House

Clandon Park

Strait of Dover

Wilton House

Uppark

Arundel Castle

Beaulieu

Castle Drogo

Osborne House

Norris Castle

The Royal Pavilion

Carisbrooke Castle

St Michael's Mount

English Channel

Kenwood House

Kensington Palace

Osterley Park

Chiswick House

Buckingham Palace

Westminster Palace

Syon House

Kew Palace

Marble Hill House

Strawberry Hill

LONDON

Hampton Court Palace

SCOTLAND, WALES
AND NORTHERN IRELAND

*Above: Balmoral Castle was Prince
Albert's fantasy Highland castle.*

SCOTLAND

 1746–89 Inveraray Castle, Argyll, rebuilt to the design of Robert Adam.

1777–92 Robert Adam works on the refurbishment of Culzean Castle, Ayrshire.

1815 William Wilkins's Dalmeny House, Lothian, is built in the Tudor Revival style.

*c.*1825 Architect William Burn's Carstairs House, Strathclyde, is built in the Elizabethan Revival style.

1855 Prince Albert completes Balmoral Castle, Grampian, in the Scottish Baronial style.

1891 A Scots Baronial east wing is added to Glamis Castle in Tayside.

1901–05 Manderston near Duns, Berwickshire, one of the finest of Edwardian country houses, is built by John Kinross for Sir James Miller.

1912 Lt-Col John MacRae-Gilstrap begins the restoration of 13th-century Eilean Donan Castle near Dornie.

1952 The Queen Mother buys and restores the Castle of Mey in Caithness.

*c.*1955 Edward Bruce, 10th Earl of Elgin, rebuilds the 17th-century Culross Abbey House in Fife.

1955 The Queen Mother adds a new wing to Birkhall near Balmoral.

1960 Claud Phillimore designs Abercairney at Crieff in Perthshire.

1938–70 Restoration of Kisimul Castle, Isle of Barra, by Robert MacNeil.

N
W E
S

Castle of Mey

North Sea

Moray Firth

Eilean Donan Castle

Balmoral Castle & Birkhall

Kisimul Castle

SCOTLAND

Glamis Castle

Duart Castle

Inverary Castle

Carstairs House

Firth of Forth

Dalmeny House

Edinburgh Castle

Manderston

Eglington Castle

North Atlantic Ocean

Culzean Castle

Solway Firth

ENGLAND

Irish Sea

Irish Sea

Plass Newydd Penrhyn Castle

Cardigan Bay

ENGLAND

WALES

Picton Castle
Cresselly House

Castell Coch Cardiff Castle

Bristol Channel

Above: Castell Coch, Wales, was remodelled by the 3rd Marquess of Bute and Burges.

WALES

1749–52 Picton Castle interior remodelled by Sir John Philipps.

1770 Cresselly House built for John Bartlett Allen.

*c.*1825 Thomas Hopper builds Penrhyn Castle in the Norman Revival style.

1866 William Burges rebuilds Cardiff Castle for the 3rd Marquess of Bute.

1875 Burges rebuilds Castell Coch, near Cardiff, for Lord Bute.

1977 John Taylor builds Castle Gyrn in Wales – a country house in castle form.

Above: Castle Coole, a fine Irish neo-classical house, was built by James Wyatt.

NORTHERN IRELAND

1790–98 James Wyatt builds Castle Coole for the 1st Earl of Belmore.

1819 Thomas Hopper begins work on Gosford Castle, Co Armagh.

*c.*1835 Edward Blore rebuilds Narrow Water Castle in the Tudor Revival style.

1867–70 Belfast Castle is built in the Scots Baronial style.

1824 The Argory, Moy, a neoclassical house, built for Walter McGeough.

Hezlett House North Channel

NORTHERN IRELAND

Barons Court

Belfast Castle

The Argory

Ballywater Park

Mount Stewart

Florence Court Castle Coole

Gosford Castle

Castle Ward

Narrow Water Castle

IRELAND

Irish Sea

13

THE MONARCHS

This list of monarchs names the kings and queens of Britain from the time of the ancient rulers of England and Scotland to the present-day reign of the royal House of Windsor.

Much of the modern monarchy's authority and prestige derives from its ancient roots and from the centuries of historical continuity celebrated in the genealogical and dynastic tables shown here. However there are countless examples of force of arms and political manoeuvring intervening in dynastic or designated succession. Following the death of Queen Anne, Prince George of Brunswick-Lüneburg, Elector of Hanover, acceded to the throne under the terms of the 1701 Act of Settlement. The Jacobite rebellions of 1715 and 1745 challenged the position of the Crown but ultimately ended in failure. The House of Hanover gave Britain two of her most notorious kings: George III who lost Britain her North American colonies and descended into madness, and his son George IV, the Prince Regent, whose extravagant and flamboyant lifestyle inspired the period known as the Regency and brought the monarchy into disrepute.

Throughout these and many other upheavals, the theory of dynastic succession was maintained. These tables trace the royal family from the accession of the German king George I in 1714 through the development of the worldwide British Empire under Victoria to the long reign of Elizabeth II.

In the last 200 years, political power has passed from the monarch to Parliament. Victoria's reign saw the establishment of the monarchy as a well-respected British institution. Many of the royal scandals of the 20th century, from the abdication crisis onwards, have damaged that reputation, but even today the monarchy remains a fundamental force in British life.

KINGS AND QUEENS OF SCOTLAND (TO 1603)

THE HOUSE OF MACALPINE
Kenneth I mac Alpin 841–859
Donald I 859–863
Constantine I 863–877
Aed Whitefoot 877–878
Eochaid 878–889 (joint)
Giric 878–889
Donald II Dasachtach 889–900
Constantine II 900–943
Malcolm I 943–954
Indulf 954–962
Dubh 962–967
Culen 967–971
Kenneth II 971–995
Constantine III 995–997
Kenneth III 997–1005
Malcolm II 1005–1034

THE HOUSE OF DUNKELD
Duncan I 1034–1040
Macbeth 1040–1057
Lulach 1057–1058
Malcolm III Canmore 1058–1093
Donald III 1093–1094
Duncan II 1094
Donald III 1094–1097 (joint)

Above: James IV of Scotland presenting arms to his wife Queen Margaret, daughter of King Henry VII of England.

Edmund 1094–1097 (joint)
Edgar 1097–1107
Alexander I 1107–1124
David I 1124–1153
Malcolm IV the Maiden 1153–1165
William I the Lion 1165–1214
Alexander II 1214–1249
Alexander III 1249–1286
Margaret, Maid of Norway 1286–1290

THE HOUSE OF BALLIOL
John Balliol 1292–1296

THE HOUSE OF BRUCE
Robert I the Bruce 1306–1329
David II 1329–1332, 1338–1371

THE HOUSE OF BALLIOL
Edward Balliol 1332–1336

THE HOUSE OF STEWART
Robert II 1371–1390
Robert III 1390–1406
James I 1406–1437
James II 1437–1460
James III 1460–1488
James IV 1488–1513
James V 1513–1542
Mary, Queen of Scots 1542–1567
James VI 1567–1603

Below: King David II of Scotland (left) makes peace with King Edward III of England, in 1357.

KINGS AND QUEENS OF ENGLAND

THE HOUSE OF WESSEX
Egbert (802–839)
Aethelwulf (839–858)
Aethelbald (858–860)
Aethelbert (860–865/6)
Aethelred I (865/6–871)
Alfred the Great (871–899)
Edward the Elder (899–924/5)
Athelstan (924/5–939)
Edmund I (939–946)
Eadred (946–955)
Eadwig (955–959)
Edgar (959–975)
Edward the Martyr (975–978)
Aethelred II the Unready (978–1013, 1014–1016)
Edmund Ironside (1016)

THE DANISH LINE
Cnut (1016–1035)
Harald I Hardrada (1035–1040)
Harthacnut (1040–1042)

THE HOUSE OF WESSEX, RESTORED
Edward the Confessor (1042–1066)
Harold II (1066)

THE NORMANS
William I the Conqueror (1066–1087)
William II Rufus (1087–1100)
Henry I (1100–1135)
Stephen (1135–1154)

Above: King John goes riding. Hunting was the sport of kings from William I.

THE PLANTAGENETS
Henry II (1154–1189)
Richard I the Lionheart (1189–1199)
John (1199–1216)
Henry III (1216–1272)
Edward I (1272–1307)
Edward II (1307–1327)
Edward III (1327–1377)
Richard II (1377–1399)

THE HOUSE OF LANCASTER
Henry IV (1399–1413)
Henry V (1413–1422)
Henry VI (1422–1461, 1470–1471)

THE HOUSE OF YORK
Edward IV (1461–1470, 1471–1483)
Edward V (1483)
Richard III (1483–1485)

THE HOUSE OF TUDOR
Henry VII (1485–1509)
Henry VIII (1509–1547)
Edward VI (1547–1553)
Lady Jane Grey (1553)
Mary I (1553–1558)
Elizabeth I (1558–1603)

Left: The heraldic badges of Kings Edward III, Richard II and Henry IV from Writhe's Garter Book.

KINGS AND QUEENS OF GREAT BRITAIN

THE HOUSE OF STUART
James I (1603-1625)
Charles I (1625-1649)
Charles II (1660-1685)
James II (1685-1688)
William III and Mary II (1689-1694)
William III (1689-1702)
Anne (1702-1714)

THE HOUSE OF HANOVER
George I (1714-1727)
George II (1727-1760)
George III (1760-1820)
George IV (1820-1830)
William IV (1830-1837)
Victoria (1837-1901)

THE HOUSE OF SAXE-COBURG-GOTHA
Edward VII (1901-1910)

THE HOUSE OF WINDSOR
George V (1910-1936)
Edward VIII (1936)
George VI (1936-1952)
Elizabeth II (1952-)

Below: The Archbishop of Canterbury reverently places the crown on George V's head at the coronation in 1911.

CHAPTER ONE

THE BAROQUE AND PALLADIAN STYLES

*c.*1714–*c.*1760

Soldier, playwright and London socialite, John Vanbrugh, had no experience of building when, in 1699, in association with Nicholas Hawksmoor, he began to draw up designs for the grand and exuberant Castle Howard in Yorkshire. Starting from scratch as an architect, his revolutionary great house – a group of buildings full of energy and movement – was designed to be seen as a vast sculpture against garden structures and ornaments in a great landscape. It was the first major statement of the Baroque in English architecture.

The often sensuous and dramatic Baroque style in art and architecture had developed from *c.*1600 in continental Europe, particularly in the strongly Roman Catholic countries of Italy and Spain. As it spread to Protestant countries, including England, it found expression in monumental and highly ornamented buildings set in grand, picturesque landscapes. Vanbrugh went on, with Hawksmoor, to design and build another great Baroque house, Blenheim Palace.

However, to some early 18th-century architects and patrons, the Baroque style seemed overblown. These men looked back to more sober classical buildings designed almost a century earlier by Inigo Jones, under the influence of the Italian Renaissance architect and theorist, Andrea Palladio. Led by Colen Campbell, Richard Boyle, 3rd Earl of Burlington, and William Kent, the Palladian movement resulted in the building of more restrained houses on the villa plan, such as Campbell's Mereworth Castle and Wanstead, Lord Burlington's Chiswick House and Kent's Holkham Hall.

Left: Castle Howard's crowning glory is its majestic dome and lantern. Vanbrugh and Hawksmoor added the feature to their design after building had begun in 1699.

CASTLE HOWARD
VANBRUGH'S MASTERPIECE

The immensely proud Charles Howard, 3rd Earl of Carlisle, had the opportunity to make a grand architectural statement when his centuries-old family mansion, Henderskelfe Castle in Yorkshire, was severely damaged by fire in 1693. He called on one of the leading architects of his day, William Talman, to draw up plans. But the men quarrelled over the architect's proposed charges, and Lord Carlisle dismissed Talman. Then he made an astonishing decision, entrusting the vast project to John Vanbrugh, a rising playwright and man-about-town in London. Vanbrugh had already proved himself a brilliant man, but there was clearly no way of knowing whether he could apply his abilities to architecture.

Vanbrugh turned to his friend, the architect Nicholas Hawksmoor, for help and also worked closely with Lord Carlisle himself on the house. Credit for the exuberant Baroque masterpiece they created is usually given to Vanbrugh but should really be shared by all three. The first designs were made in 1699, and building – using a delightful pale yellow local stone – began in 1700.

Below: Vanbrugh's Temple of the Four Winds was unfinished at his death in 1726. It was completed in 1738. Francesco Vassalli decorated the inside with scagliola.

ENGLAND'S FIRST DOME
The main entrance front faces north. Beneath an imposing dome, its grand central block is faced with Corinthian pilasters and contains elegant arched doorways and windows; statues and urns occupy niches and stand on the balustrade. The magnificent dome and lantern, the first in England, was completed by 1706, predating the dome of St Paul's Cathedral, London, by two years. However, the dome visible today is actually a meticulous 20th-century reconstruction, built after the original dome was destroyed in a fire of 1940.

EAST AND WEST WINGS
Wings to the west and east were intended to extend forward to create a grand forecourt. The east wing was built by Vanbrugh and Hawksmoor, and beyond it is a second service enclosure, the Laundry Court. The original design called for a similar structure on the west side, but the western wing was not built, because Lord Carlisle lost interest in the project. (The west wing we see today was added in 1759 in the Palladian style by Sir Thomas Robinson.)

Above: Beauty, energy, exuberance, drama. Thanks to renovation, Castle Howard still has the magnificent profile its creators envisaged. The Atlas Fountain (foreground) was added by the 7th Earl in the 1850s.

The south, or garden, front also makes dramatic use of Corinthian pilasters: here smaller ones on the single-storey wings echo the large and impressive ones on the two-storey main block. The whole front has a rusticated basement with square windows that contrast with the arched ones above them.

THE ESSENCE OF THE BAROQUE
Inside, the hugely impressive entrance hall is 52ft (16m) square and is lit from the lantern in the dome, which rises to a height of 70ft (21m) overhead. Two staircases and four stone corridors lead off, creating a sense of movement through a dramatic use of architectural space that exemplifies the finest qualities of the English Baroque.

The hall frescoes and the decoration within the dome were painted by the Italian artist Giovanni Pellegrini in 1709–12. The fireplace and Niche of

Bacchus were made of *scagliola* (a combination of marble and plaster) by Italian craftsmen Bagutti and Plura in 1711–12. It is one of the earliest examples in England of the craft, which became very popular later in the century.

The largest of the other rooms is now the Long Gallery in the west wing, though prior to a fire in 1940 some of the many staterooms on the south front were grander. Left unfinished for 50 years, the gallery was completed by Charles Tatham *c*.1810. This wing also contained the main bedrooms.

DESIGNING THE GROUNDS

In the early 1720s, with the house inhabitable but the west wing not started, Lord Carlisle became more interested in setting out the gardens and park with pavilions and 'rustic' buildings than in completing the house to the original designs. Vanbrugh and Hawksmoor continued to work on these projects at Castle Howard until their deaths, in 1726 and 1736 respectively.

In the grounds, Vanbrugh designed the domed Temple of the Four Winds, originally known as the Temple of Diana and partly based on Andrea Palladio's Villa Capra near Vicenza (the same house that inspired Colen Campbell's Mereworth Castle). The temple was built in 1723–38.

The cylindrical mausoleum for the burial of Lord Carlisle and his descendants, the grandest in Britain, was

Above: Eighteenth-century promenaders admire Castle Howard's south front.

originally designed by Hawksmoor in 1729, although his plan was significantly altered in the 1730s by others, including Sir Thomas Robinson and Lord Burlington. In addition to the vaults, it contains a chapel with a graceful domed ceiling. It was finished in the 1740s. Hawksmoor based his design on that of the 1502 Church of St Pietro in Montorio in Rome, designed by Donato Bramante for Pope Julius II.

The grounds also contain an obelisk, erected in 1714, at the head of the drive where the great lime avenues intersect; a pyramid designed by Hawksmoor in 1728; a gatehouse that was originally a freestanding 'pyramid arch' designed by

Vanbrugh in 1719, but which had wings added by Sir Thomas Robinson in 1756-8; and mock fortifications in the style of medieval town walls, erected near the gatehouse in the 1720s.

DRAMATIC SETTING

Building these structures in the grounds was part of the architects' original conception, for they wanted to create the most dramatic of settings for their imposing house. Horace Walpole, connoisseur and creator of Strawberry Hill at Twickenham, visited Castle Howard in 1772. His reaction would doubtless have delighted Hawksmoor, Vanbrugh and Lord Carlisle, for he enthused about its sublime environs as much as the house itself: 'Nobody…had informed me that I should at one view see a palace, a town, a fortified city, temples on high places, woods worthy of being each a metropolis of the Druids, vales connected to hills by other woods, the noblest lawn in the world fenced by half the horizon, and a mausoleum that would tempt one to be buried alive; in short I have seen gigantic palaces before but never a sublime one.'

THE ENGLISH BAROQUE

The word 'baroque' denoted works of art that ignored the accepted proportions or rules. Paintings, sculpture and architecture by great Baroque artists, such as the Italian Gian Lorenzo Bernini, were sensuous and dramatic, aiming to appeal to the soul by way of the senses. When the style was taken up in Protestant northern Europe, it tended to be more formal and restrained, appealing to viewers through its monumental size,

surface ornamentation, the geometric arrangement of its constituent parts and its interaction with its setting, be it the streets around a London church or a picturesque country park around a stately house. Some historians see the English version of the Baroque as springing fully formed from Vanbrugh and Hawksmoor at Castle Howard; others argue that it had its antecedent a little earlier in Hawksmoor's Easton Neston.

BLENHEIM PALACE
AND THE MARLBOROUGHS

In 1705, Queen Anne gave the royal manor of Woodstock near Oxford to John Churchill, 1st Duke of Marlborough. The land was to be the setting for a great mansion, a lasting tribute from a grateful queen and country for Marlborough's victory over a French-Bavarian army in August 1704, at Blenheim, in southern Germany.

To build the great house that would become known as Blenheim Palace, the Duke chose John Vanbrugh. In doing so he overlooked the more obvious claim of Sir Christopher Wren, Surveyor of the Queen's Works and the choice of Marlborough's strong-willed and powerful wife, Sarah. As a result, Vanbrugh and the Duchess got off to a bad start, and they were at odds throughout the building, much of which took place while the Duke himself was away at war.

With Nicholas Hawksmoor, Vanbrugh set out to build a monument to the Duke's great victories and the age of Queen Anne, a Baroque mansion that placed enormous emphasis on style and grandeur. The Duchess, however, wanted a country house designed for comfort.

ROYAL DISFAVOUR

Building began in 1705. The arguments between Vanbrugh and the Duchess were compounded by major problems in paying for materials and labour: costs were supposedly to be covered by the Queen and the state but money was often not forthcoming, particularly after the Marlboroughs lost favour with the Queen and retreated into continental exile in 1712. Work at Blenheim ceased that year, with the workforce owed £45,000. After Anne's death in 1714, the Duke and Duchess returned and work resumed on the house. But after a major row with the Duchess, Vanbrugh resigned in fury in 1717, and Hawksmoor worked on alone. The great house was largely completed by 1722, the year of the Duke's death, but this brought no

Above: Aristocratic breeding. Churchill (left), with wife, Lady Sarah, and five children.

end to the animosity between the Duchess and Vanbrugh. In 1725, he was even refused entrance by the Duchess when he attempted to visit with the Earl of Carlisle to view his work.

THE GREAT COURT

Everywhere at Blenheim, the scale is vast. The house's main entrance stands beneath a towering portico bearing the Duke's arms on the pediment, amid the extravagantly ornamented splendour of the Great Court. On either side of the portico are curved arcades; the four corners of the 480ft (145m) wide central block are topped with extraordinary towers bearing pinnacles 30ft (9m) high carved by Grinling Gibbons. Tuscan colonnades connect the house to the service and stable courts. Enclosed by these side wings, the Great Court is no less than 300ft (90m) deep.

A long straight drive leads directly into the Great Court, but modern visitors enter through the East Gate in the wall of the service court, and then through another fine gateway beneath the clock tower into the Great Court. The house's plainer, and perhaps more elegant, south front contains another great portico topped with a 30-ton marble bust of Louis XIV. This was a spoil of war that the Duke had taken from Tournai in 1709.

SIR JOHN VANBRUGH

Vanbrugh was born in 1664 and served as a soldier, 1686–98. He was imprisoned in the Bastille in Paris as a spy. He came to eminence as a playwright in London, with *The Relapse* and *The Provok'd Wife*, and mixed with great men of the day in the Kit Cat Club, where he met Lord Carlisle, who commissioned him to design his first house, Castle Howard in Yorkshire. Vanbrugh worked with Nicholas Hawksmoor on Castle Howard, Blenheim Palace, and Kimbolton Castle. Working alone, he built Kings Weston House in Gloucestershire, Eastbury in Dorset and Seaton Delaval Hall in Northumberland – the last regarded as another great masterpiece. His final work was the north front of Grimsthorpe Castle, Lincolnshire (1722–6). Vanbrugh

Above: Sir John Vanbrugh, engraved by artist John Simon (c.1675–1751).

served as Comptroller of Royal Works under Anne and George I. Until his death in 1726, he worked for Carlisle at Castle Howard, where his Temple of the Four Winds was completed after his death.

THE GREAT HALL

Blenheim's interior was designed on a correspondingly vast scale and decorated by the finest craftsmen. Behind the entrance portico stands the Great Hall – 67ft (20m) high, with vast Corinthian columns and tall arches, beneath a painted ceiling, by Sir James Thornhill, of Marlborough showing a map of Blenheim battlefield and being rewarded by Britannia with a laurel wreath. The hall leads into the Saloon, decorated with heroic murals and ceiling by Louis Laguerre and also featuring magnificent marble door frames by Hawksmoor. From the Saloon, a great room leads off on either side; these rooms were originally state apartments but were later turned into drawing rooms.

The last part of the house to be completed was the west wing. It contains the splendid Long Library, 180ft (55m) long, designed as a picture gallery but finished by Hawksmoor as a library, and the chapel, featuring a grand marble tomb designed by William Kent and carved by John Michael Rysbrack to hold the remains of the Duke and Duchess.

GARDEN AND PARKLAND

As at Castle Howard, Vanbrugh and Hawksmoor devoted as much attention to the setting of Blenheim as to its façades and interior. On the south side,

Right: In the Red Drawing Room hangs a portrait of the 9th Duke and his American heiress wife, Consuelo Vanderbilt.

a monumental parterre was laid out by Henry Wise, gardener at Hampton Court. A 134ft (41m) column of Victory, raised to celebrate the Duke's military triumphs, stands at the end of an avenue of elms planted to recall the arrangement of Marlborough's soldiers at the Battle of Blenheim. Vanbrugh channelled the River Glyme into three streams and built a vast bridge across them; the bridge was partly submerged when 'Capability' Brown landscaped the park in the 1760s and created a lake in place of the streams.

BAROQUE EMBODIMENT

The great house in its carefully orchestrated setting aims throughout for an impression of power, a celebration of great English victories and the military prowess of Marlborough himself: an embodiment that was, in Vanbrugh's words, a

Above: An aerial view allows the eye to take in the complete composition, with 300ft (90m)- deep enclosure and colonnades linking to the east and west courts.

creation of 'beauty, magnificence and duration'. Such an achievement is not to everyone's taste, however. Even when it was newly finished, the great palace was not universally approved. At a time when the classical Palladian movement was gathering force, Blenheim appeared to many as heavy, indulgent and overblown. But others have seen it as the highest and fullest expression of the English Baroque, an achievement, according to Sir John Soane, architect of the Bank of England in 1788, that proves Vanbrugh (and perhaps, in truth, also Hawksmoor) to have been no less than 'the Shakespeare of architects'.

MEREWORTH CASTLE
AND PALLADIAN HOUSES

The elegant Mereworth Castle in Kent, a domed rectangular block with a classical portico on each of its four sides, is a recreation of the mid-16th-century Villa Capra, or Rotonda, built by Andrea Palladio near Vicenza in Italy. Built by the Scottish architect Colen Campbell in 1720–3, Mereworth is one of the finest early examples of the Palladian movement in 18th-century English architecture (the first in England being Wilbury House in Wiltshire, built *c.*1710 by William Benson).

ROMAN STYLE

'Palladianism' takes its name from Andrea Palladio (1508–80), who, as well as being the architect and designer of elegant villas and churches, was an interpreter of classical building and, in particular, of the work of 1st-century BC Roman architect, Vitruvius. Palladio's illustrated volume, the *Four Books of Architecture*, first published in 1570, was reissued in a lavish English edition in London in 1715, at a time when – following the accession of King George I in 1714 – many of the wealthy elite of Georgian England, who had often travelled widely in Italy, were turning away from the prevailing taste for

Below: Palladio in England. This elevation of Mereworth Castle was published in Colen Campbell's Vitruvius Britannicus *(1724).*

extravagantly ornate houses and developing an enthusiasm for more restrained, classical buildings.

The 'Palladians' looked back to the buildings of Inigo Jones, who, almost a century earlier, had tried to put the principles of Palladio into practice in the Queen's House, Greenwich, and the Banqueting House, Whitehall. Following Palladio, they believed buildings should be constructed 'rationally' in line with the principles of proportion, symmetry and harmony found in the natural world.

One of the leading Palladians was the architect of Mereworth Castle, Colen Campbell, who, also in 1715, published his *Vitruvius Britannicus* – a survey of classical buildings in England. In the introduction he praised 'great Palladio' and dismissed the Baroque artist, Bernini, as 'affected and licentious'.

PALLADIANISM AT MEREWORTH

Mereworth Castle is a triumph of elegant design. Its dome is encased in lead and contains 24 chimneys that pass through its shell to exit via a single opening at the top. Beneath the dome is a delightful circular hall, called the Saloon by Campbell, measuring 35ft

Above: Campbell built Stourhead House, Wiltshire, in the 1720s. Note the statues above the pedimented portico. The side pavilions were added in the 1790s.

(11m) in diameter and 80ft (24m) high, and lit from above by windows in the base of the dome. It has terracotta walls decorated with stucco in the form of foliage and graceful reclining figures. An extremely refined drawing room fills the whole length of the south front. A spiral staircase leads to a circular gallery at first-floor level that looks over the hall.

Below: Stourhead gardens were designed by Henry Home II in 1741–80 and inspired by the landscapes of Poussin and Claude.

The villa stands on a mound in a broad valley and was, until the late 1800s, surrounded by a moat. The moat was a hangover from the original castle on the site, inherited and redeveloped by Campbell's patron John Fane, after 1736 the 7th Earl of Westmorland. The two graceful pavilions that flank the entrance front of Campbell's villa were added in the late 1730s, probably by James Stuart.

OTHER PALLADIAN HOUSES

Before he began work at Mereworth Castle in 1720, Campbell had already designed and started building (c.1714) a

Below: The 3rd Earl of Burlington's Chiswick House (now in west London) was based on the same Palladian villa at Vicenza that Campbell recreated at Mereworth Castle.

big influential Palladian villa at Wanstead House in Essex, as well as creating, in 1717, the first Palladian façade in London for Burlington House, Piccadilly, home of Richard Boyle, 3rd Earl of Burlington, himself a key figure in the Palladian movement. In addition, he built Stourhead House, in Wiltshire (c.1717–25), for banker Henry Hoare and later worked alongside James Gibbs at Houghton Hall, in Norfolk, from c.1722.

Several Palladian houses were built at this time. The 3rd Earl of Burlington, Campbell's patron for Burlington House, built his own Palladian villa,

Above: The Palladian bridge at Prior Park was part of a landscape garden created by Bath entrepreneur Ralph Allen.

Chiswick House (now in west London), beginning in 1725. Burlington's protégé, the painter William Kent, turned architect in 1734 when he designed Holkham Hall in Norfolk with Lord Leicester, another influential figure in the Palladian revival. Finally, in 1735–48, John Wood the Elder built Prior Park, near Bath, with gardens created by Ralph Allen and advice from poet Alexander Pope and 'Capability' Brown.

WANSTEAD HOUSE

Colen Campbell began work in 1715 on Wanstead House in Essex for banker, Sir Richard Child, later Earl Tylney. Now demolished, the house was a Palladian villa of significant size, measuring 260 x 70ft (79 x 21m), and was graced by a classical portico with a pediment 60ft (18m) wide and six Corinthian columns. It was built on the site of an earlier mansion Sir Richard inherited from his half-brother, Sir Josiah Child. Leading gardener George London developed the grounds.

Right: Wanstead House had a lavish ballroom, which is seen at its finest in this 'conversation piece' by William Hogarth.

HOLKHAM HALL
AND WILLIAM KENT

The stately Holkham Hall, near Wells in Norfolk, built after 1734 by William Kent and Matthew Brettingham, with copious advice from Lord Burlington and especially Thomas Coke, the Earl of Leicester, is celebrated as the most distinguished of all the great Palladian houses in England. Its coolly magnificent Marble Hall, which Kent and Leicester designed along the lines of a Roman basilica and which contains tall Ionic columns of alabaster, makes an unforgettable impression on all who see it.

The house consists of a rectangular central block containing the Marble Hall and staterooms, and four 'wings', one attached to each corner of the rectangle, containing visitors' apartments, family rooms, a chapel and kitchens. The wing containing the family rooms, which included the elegant Long Library, could be used as a self-contained house when Leicester was not entertaining in style and did not need the staterooms.

AUSTERE SOUTH FRONT

Holkham Hall's principal south, or garden, front is much discussed, for it takes Palladian restraint and distaste for ornament to the point of austere plainness. It is 344ft (105m) across, including the south-west and south-east

wings at the sides. In the centre rises a portico with six tall columns; towers project at the corners of the main block, each containing an arched three-light Venetian window on the *piano nobile* (the first floor, containing the principal apartments). Above these – and above the four square windows that are aligned horizontally across the front – rises an expanse of plain yellow brickwork where the eye might normally expect to see further windows or architectural ornament.

Above: The wide south front at Holkham, with its six-column portico, looks across formal gardens (designed in the 1850s by Nesfield).

Beneath the *piano nobile* is a rusticated basement containing small, functional windows. The overall effect borders on the severe – a precise study in symmetry and proportion.

Below: Elegant proportions, beautiful symmetry. Kent and Leicester created a vast Palladian house at Holkham in windswept Norfolk.

ARCHITECT AS DESIGNER

The house's interior is comparatively lavish, but even its richest interiors are handled with a fine Palladian sense of restraint. The ravishingly elegant Marble Hall rises to a height of 50ft (15m) and contains a wide flight of marble steps. These climb to a peristyle forming a gallery, off which lead doorways to the state rooms. Classical influences abound: the gilded ceiling is taken from an Inigo Jones design that was copied from the Pantheon in Rome; the fluted columns of Derbyshire marble are derived from those in the Roman Temple of Fortuna Virilis.

The staterooms are grandly elegant and display paintings and statuary acquired by Coke during a famous and extended Grand Tour of 1712–18. Beyond the hall is the Saloon, with gilded ceiling and door surrounds and velvet-lined walls. The Statue Gallery, which leads across the house from south to north, houses Coke's fine classical statues in curved niches – including an ancient Greek bust of Athenian aristocrat and historian, Thucydides, dating to *c*.4BC. The rooms are furnished with velvet-covered chairs and sofas, as well as side tables, all designed by Kent (at Holkham, he pioneered a new role for the architect as designer of all aspects of the patron's living space). He also designed fine interiors for the family rooms in the south-west wing, especially in the Long Library.

HOLKHAM'S STYLE

Other men also had a significant input into the house's appearance. These were Thomas Coke himself and Kent's chief patron and the great promoter of the Palladian style, Lord Burlington, as well as the Norfolk architect Matthew Brettingham, who was Clerk of Works on the project and later a competent architect with a good practice.

Right: Badminton House, Gloucestershire, where Kent reworked an earlier house in the Palladian style. This view is by Canaletto.

WILLIAM KENT

William Kent excelled as an architect, and as an interior and garden designer. He began as a painter, and while studying painting in Rome in 1709–19 he met his great patrons Richard Boyle, 3rd Earl of Burlington, and Thomas Coke, later Earl of Leicester. In 1719, he formed a lifelong association with Burlington when he decorated Burlington House in Piccadilly, London. Burlington secured Kent the position of Master Carpenter in the Office of Works in 1725, and in this capacity he rebuilt the stable block of King's Mews, Charing Cross, in 1732. (Now demolished, it stood on the site of the National Gallery in Trafalgar Square.)

William Kent also designed the Treasury Buildings and built the Horse Guards Building, both in Whitehall. As well as designing Holkham Hall, he was also architect of Badminton House, Gloucestershire. He designed interiors for Ditchley Park, Oxfordshire, and furnishings for Hampton Court Palace. As a garden designer, his work at Rousham

Above: William Kent's ability as a garden designer and interior decorator probably outshone his skill as an architect.

Park and Stowe House led a movement away from formal French-style gardens into informal 'natural' landscapes of the kind that would be further developed later in the century by 'Capability' Brown. He died in 1748.

Plans for the house may have first been conceived by Coke, Burlington and Kent when they met in Rome in 1715. Holkham Hall was not begun until 1734, however, largely because Coke lost a fortune in the collapse of the South Sea Company in 1720. Building work then carried on for 30 years until 1764, after the deaths of Kent (1748), Burlington (1753) and Leicester

himself (1759). The house was dutifully completed by the Earl's widow – Lady Margaret, Baroness Clifford.

The park at Holkham, among the largest in England, contains an obelisk designed by Kent and erected before the house was built, in 1729. Formal avenues were created, but the park was landscaped by 'Capability' Brown later in the 18th century.

DITCHLEY PARK
AND JAMES GIBBS

The country house of Ditchley Park, near Oxford, is celebrated less for its exterior of weathered Burford stone and beautiful parkland setting, than for its elegant and well-preserved interiors designed by William Kent and Henry Flitcroft in the 1720s. It is also well known for its role in World War II, when it served as the weekend HQ for Winston Churchill and his War Cabinet in 1940–2, at a time when the Prime Minister's country residence at Chequers, in Buckinghamshire, was under threat of being bombed.

INELEGANT ROOFLINE

The house was designed and built not by Kent but by James Gibbs in 1722. His patron was George Henry Lee, 2nd Earl of Lichfield and grandson of King Charles II, and his mistress Barbara Villiers, Duchess of Cleveland. It consists of a central block connected to two perfectly symmetrical wings by curved colonnades. The main block has a truncated appearance, for its two main

Below: Gibbs's design for Ditchley Park inspired that of Arundel Park, Sussex, in the 1950s, which in turn began a revival of Palladianism in the later 20th century.

JAMES GIBBS: FAVOURED ARCHITECT OF TORY LORDS

Born in Aberdeenshire in 1682, James Gibbs studied in Rome and in his early career was an Italian Baroque architect. In this style he designed the Church of St Mary-le-Strand in London in 1714–17. But he was influenced by the prevailing enthusiasm for 'Palladianism' and began to mix classical and Baroque elements as in his celebrated Church of St-Martin-in-the-Fields, London (1722–6), which has both classical portico and towering steeple and was copied for churches throughout Britain and North America.

He was also a successful and influential country-house architect. He designed or contributed to at least 50 houses. While Vanbrugh was a favourite of the Whig

Right: A Baroque Palladian? Gibbs's designs for both country houses and churches were highly influential.

nobility, Gibbs was the leading architect employed by Tories. His *Book of Architecture* (1728) was widely used as a pattern book. He was also a favourite at England's leading universities, designing the Senate House at Cambridge University (1722–30) and the Radcliffe Camera for Oxford University (1737–49).

floors, equipped with gracefully tall windows, are topped with a squat third level and an unsuccessful roofline with poorly positioned statues of Fortune and Fame and inelegant chimneys. Architectural historians point out that

Gibbs' original designs proposed the use of either a pediment and cupolas or a columned portico, and speculate that the final design must have been the result of a sudden shortage of funds when building was underway. The two wings, however, are very attractive: each has ten windows in the façade, a hipped roof and a clock tower.

ELEGANT INTERIORS

Ditchley Park's interiors are superb examples of early Georgian elegance. The entrance leads into a central hall two storeys high: its walls carry busts of leading philosophers and writers; carved embodiments of the Arts and the Sciences recline above the doorway into the Saloon, the splendid fireplace and the alcove opposite it; the hall ceiling was painted by Kent; and the Saloon contains a riot of Italian stucco work.

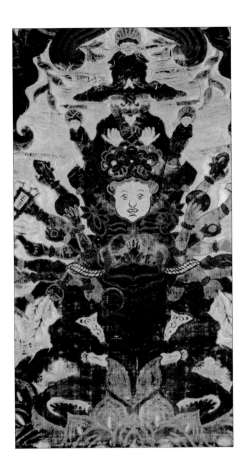

Above: A decidedly Eastern influence is evident in the design of this furnishing silk of 1738, which is hung at Ditchley Park.

Furniture and works of art are of the highest quality: in the White Drawing Room are two very fine eagle tables designed by Kent, and portraits by Sir Peter Lely of Charles II and Barbara Villiers. The house's chimney-pieces – always the most expensive items in decorative schemes – are by Christopher Horsenail and Henry Cheere.

AMERICAN CONNECTIONS

The house passed from the 2nd Earl of Lichfield through many generations of Dillon-Lee descendants until 1932,

when the 17th Viscount Dillon sold it. One branch of the Oxfordshire Lees settled in Virginia, where their most famous son was Confederate commander, Robert E. Lee.

In 1932, another American came to the rescue of Ditchley Park. He was Ronald Tree, a former managing editor of *Forum Magazine* in New York, who later became MP for Harborough, Leicestershire. With his wife, Nancy, also an American, he modernized the house and restored the garden. He came to

Left: Intricate beauty. This side table, elegantly designed by Kent, is part of the interior decor at Ditchley Park.

Above: The entrance hall at Ditchley. Note the ceiling painting by Kent and the busts of thinkers and writers arrayed around the walls.

know Churchill and agreed to the Prime Minister's request that leading Cabinet members might use Ditchley Park as a weekend HQ.

In the 1950s, David Wills bought the house and presented it to the Anglo-American Ditchley Foundation, which holds international conferences for invited academics, politicians, business people, industrialists and civil servants to further international understanding. The house is periodically open to the general public, subject to booking.

HOUGHTON HALL
AND SIR ROBERT WALPOLE

England's first prime minister, Robert Walpole, used Colen Campbell, James Gibbs and Thomas Ripley as architects and William Kent as interior designer in building the sumptuous Houghton Hall, near King's Lynn, Norfolk, in 1722–35. Walpole eschewed the Norfolk brick later used by his near-neighbour at Holkham Hall, and built his country house of fine Aislaby sandstone from Yorkshire, expensively transported by sea from Whitby to King's Lynn.

Robert Walpole had inherited a relatively small Jacobean manor house and estate at Houghton in 1700, at the age of 24, on the death of his father. In the same year he began his political life, when he was elected Member of Parliament for his father's seat of Castle Rising, Norfolk. After making an enormous fortune as Minister at War, Walpole began the building of a grand new house on the estate in 1722, by which time the politician had become Chancellor of the Exchequer and First Lord of the Admiralty.

Below: The rose garden at Houghton Hall contains 150 varieties of the species.

Above: The entrance front, Houghton Hall. Note the standing statues above the portico, the double staircase and the side colonnades.

RESTRAINED EXTERIOR

The house has a coolly elegant Palladian exterior. The original design, by Colen Campbell, was reproduced in his *Vitruvius Britannicus* and called for a rectangular block with a tower at each corner, although the towers were replaced on James Gibbs' advice with four domes. The garden front has a grand double staircase and four-column portico beneath a carved pediment topped with three standing statues. Fine curving colonnades lead off at the sides to the wings, which contain a kitchen on one side and the one-time Picture Gallery on the other. On the entrance front, statues of Britannia and Neptune, carved by the great John Michael Rysbrack, rest above the central window.

Below: Sir Robert Walpole. He was father of Horace Walpole, builder of Strawberry Hill.

Above: Colen Campbell's design for Houghton was improved by James Gibbs's addition of domes on the four corner towers.

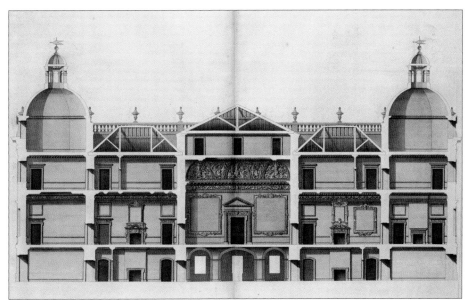

Above: A cross-section shows Campbell's design for the cube-shaped Stone Hall, with state rooms either side on the piano nobile.

SUMPTUOUS INTERIORS

The interiors are far more richly decorated than the restrained façades. Everywhere, especially in the Great Staircase, there is a profusion of mahogany, at that time only recently and expensively introduced to England. The staircase climbs stylishly to the staterooms on the *piano nobile*; the walls above the stairs are painted by Kent. Chief among the staterooms is the sumptuous Stone Hall: an elegant 40ft (12m) cube, lined with ashlar, it has a superb fireplace by Rysbrack and an extravagant stucco ceiling by Artari. The hall contains a marble bust of Sir Robert, again by Rysbrack, and a portrait of the great man by John Wootton. It also contains a bronze carving of the ancient Greek seer-priest, Laocoon, by the Frenchman François Girardon, which was given to Sir Robert by the Pope. The elegant chairs designed by William Kent are covered in their original velvet.

This is only one of many magnificent rooms in the house, for everywhere the immense wealth of Sir Robert is displayed. The Green Velvet Bedchamber contains an elaborate bed, designed by Kent, with a cockleshell headboard and green velvet hangings. The Marble Parlour, which was used as a dining room, has both a Rysbrack fireplace and serving alcoves carved from mauve and white marble, as well as portraits of Sir Robert by Jean van Loo and Sir Godfrey Kneller. The Saloon has walls lined with crimson velvet and a gold mosaic painting by Kent on its coved ceiling. It is extravagantly furnished with Kent's gilt furniture.

ARTWORKS FOR SALE

Above the chimney-piece in the Saloon hangs a portrait of Catherine the Great. In his long political career, Sir Robert amassed a magnificent collection of artworks: indeed, his group of paintings was of such size and quality that it later formed the basis of the collection of the State Hermitage Museum in St Petersburg, Russia. Sir Robert's grandson, the 3rd Earl of Orford, ran up such enormous debts that he was reduced to selling off the paintings in the late 1770s to Catherine the Great (Empress Catherine II of Russia).

The house stands in a 350-acre (142ha) park laid out by Charles Bridgeman, today occupied by a herd of white deer. The grounds contain a water tower built in 1731–3 to the designs of the 'Architect Earl', Henry Lord Herbert, subsequently 9th Earl of Pembroke. There is also a recently renovated 5 acre (2ha) walled garden with elaborate floral displays and a superb rose garden.

CHARLES BRIDGEMAN

Born in 1690, Charles Bridgeman first came to notice when working at Brompton Park Nursery in Kensington for Henry Wise. In 1726, Bridgeman was appointed joint Chief Gardener to George I with Wise, before filling the role alone on Wise's retirement the following year.

Bridgeman worked for the Prince of Wales and his mistress the Countess of Suffolk on the gardens at Marble Hill House, Twickenham. As well as laying out the grounds at Houghton Hall, he also worked on the gardens at Rousham Park, Stowe House, Chiswick House, Cliveden and Claremont.

In his capacity as royal gardener, he cared for and in places designed the royal gardens of Hampton Court, St James's Park, Windsor Castle, Richmond and Hyde Park, where he laid out the lake known as the Serpentine by damming the River Westbourne. Bridgeman also designed the elegant Round Pond in Kensington Gardens, near Kensington Palace. He died in 1738.

ROUSHAM PARK
'THE PRETTIEST PLACE'

 The beautiful grounds at Rousham Park near Steeple Aston, Oxfordshire, were laid out by royal gardener, Charles Bridgeman, in the 1720s and developed by William Kent from 1738 onward. They are one of England's first landscape gardens, and the only one in the country to survive essentially unchanged to the present.

The first house at Rousham Park was built in the Jacobean style by Sir Robert Dormer in the 1630s. It has since been much altered, but the original hall remains at the centre of the house. Sir Robert, a proud Royalist who was imprisoned during the Civil War, died in 1649. His grandson, Robert Dormer, inherited the house in 1719 and hired Bridgeman to set out the grounds.

'THE PRETTIEST PLACE'

When poet Alexander Pope, a friend of Robert Dormer, visited in 1728, he was impressed with Charles Bridgeman's work, writing that: 'Rousham is the

Above: Nature orchestrated in a vision of Arcadia at Rousham Park. A circular pond is one of the attractions in 'Venus's Vale'.

prettiest place for water-falls, jetts [sic], ponds inclosed with beautiful scenes of green and hanging wood, that ever I saw.'

Historians identify Charles Bridgeman as an early pioneer in the transition of the formal gardens of the later 17th and early 18th centuries into the 'landscape' gardens that were to be developed by William Kent and, subsequently, by 'Capability' Brown. It was Bridgeman who popularized the 'ha-ha', a concealed – usually sunken – boundary to garden or parkland that was used to make the country-house grounds appear to merge with the surrounding countryside.

THE PALLADIAN LANDSCAPE GARDEN

Palladian architects led a movement away from formal French- or Dutch-influenced gardens, with straight artificial plantings, to landscape gardens with meandering lines more like those found in nature. The landscape garden was no more natural than the formal parterres it replaced, but it was designed to look like nature – nature framed and perfected, like the vista reproduced (and perhaps slightly touched up) by a landscape artist such as Claude or Poussin. Kent and Burlington were the pioneers, creating at Chiswick House, in 1734 the first landscape garden, with wandering stream and pathways. For the Whig nobility, the straight lines of formal gardens symbolized the autocratic rule of the House of Stuart, from which England had been freed by the 'Glorious Revolution' of 1688, while the carefully produced natural appearance of the landscape garden was an image of freedom.

Left: A temple at Rousham. Roman temples and other romantic ruins appeared often in Palladian gardens.

Above: Kent designed the garden at Rousham so that a pedestrian on the winding paths would encounter a series of statues, ruins and other aesthetically pleasing 'classical' scenes.

KENT'S PICTURESQUE VISTA

Robert Dormer died in 1737 and was succeeded at Rousham by his ageing brother, James Dormer, who had served under the Duke of Marlborough and been wounded at the Battle of Blenheim in 1704. James Dormer called in William Kent in 1738 to develop the gardens further and to make alterations to the house. He set out to create visions of ancient Roman temples, statues and landscapes in the English countryside.

To the north of the house, Bridgeman's garden contained a bowling green and descending terraces that led down to the River Cherwell. Kent reworked the terraces as a smooth slope and set to work making the vista as picturesque as possible, incorporating an old mill beyond the Cherwell and a medieval bridge across the river and adding an eye-catching ruin of his own. In the woodland garden and Venus's Vale, he built temples in the style of ancient Rome, added statues and laid out circuitous paths and winding streams with ponds and artificial cascades. The whole was intended to have the appeal of a landscape painting by the then highly popular 17th-century artists, Nicolas Poussin and Claude Lorrain.

The circuitous stream Kent channelled through the Watery Walk has been claimed as the first 'serpentine' feature in garden design, the precursor of those so frequently employed in the landscaped designs of 'Capability' Brown. Kent was able to visit Rousham only infrequently, and much of the work was carried out under his direction by the estate's head gardener, John McClary, and Clerk of the Works, William White.

Kent's garden soon became an attraction for visitors. The architect-gardener had created a separate entrance for this purpose, allowing tourists to enter and view the landscape without going near the house.

PALLADIAN INTERIORS

Kent also set to work on the house, adding a battlement, cupola and very fine octagonal-paned windows (later sadly, replaced) in the entrance front. He added two wings to the house, each containing a typically elegant 'William Kent' interior: the Painted Parlour and the Library (partially altered as the Great Parlour in 1764).

In the Painted Parlour, Kent built an elaborate marble chimney-piece and over-mantel, together with wall brackets for the display of Dormer's bronzes. He also painted the mythological scene that decorates the ceiling, fitted a number of dummy doorways to provide the required symmetry and proportion, and designed the exquisite parcel-gilt chairs and gilt-wood tables. Only one element of his design is lacking: the original colour scheme, probably in gold and white, was later repainted, most recently in green *c.*1910.

In the Library, Kent constructed a ribbed and vaulted ceiling and Gothic-style cornice. The room was once lined with books, but these were removed in 1764 when Thomas Roberts transformed the Library into the Great Parlour for Jane, Lady Cottrell-Dormer, adding rococo plasterwork around portraits on the walls. In one of these frames hangs Lady Jane's portrait, by Benjamin West; that of Lt-Gen James Dormer, Kent's patron, is displayed nearby in a more restrained gilt-wood frame.

Below: The cupola was one of Kent's additions to Rousham Park. He also added the castellation to the roof, as well as building two substantial wings.

STOWE HOUSE AND GARDENS
AND THE ENGLISH PALLADIAN MOVEMENT

A colonnaded mansion set within a great park, Stowe House is a veritable English arcadia. House and gardens together form, perhaps, the finest embodiment of the English Palladian movement's vision.

Above: The Marble Saloon, beneath a dome 56ft (17m) high, was built after 1775.

Above: The Temple of Ancient Virtue is one of the classical buildings erected by Kent.

MANY ARCHITECTS

The core of the mansion was built on the site of a medieval manor house in 1676–83 by Sir Richard Temple, 3rd baronet, employing Sir Christopher Wren's master joiner, William Cleare. Stowe House was then developed in the first half of the 18th century by architects including Sir John Vanbrugh, William Kent and James Gibbs. In the same period, Stowe's original formal gardens were gradually transformed into a landscape park by the leading architect-gardeners of the day – who included Charles Bridgeman, Kent and Lancelot 'Capability' Brown. More than 30 temples and picturesque 'classical ruins' were put up in the parkland.

RENOWNED PARKLAND

Initially, the house had a parterre garden, but this was replaced in 1711–26 by a Baroque parkland designed by Vanbrugh and Bridgeman. During this period, Vanbrugh also built several structures in the park, including the Temple of Bacchus (1719), the

Doric Arch (1722) and the Egyptian Pyramid (1724–6), and he built the North Portico on the house.

Kent, Gibbs and Giacomo Leoni, publisher of Palladio's *Four Books of Architecture* in English, worked at Stowe in the 1730s-40s. Kent built the two-tiered South Portico on the house *c.*1734 and the Temple of Venus (*c.*1731), the Temple of British Worthies (*c.*1735) and the Temple of Ancient Virtue (*c.*1736); he laid out the 'Elysian Fields' and applied the 'natural' landscaping techniques developed at Rousham to the parkland.

Lancelot 'Capability' Brown was head gardener in 1741–50 and laid out the

'Grecian Valley', building the Grecian Temple (later called the Temple of Concord and Victory) in 1747. He reworked Charles Bridgeman's more formal 'Eleven-Acre Lake' and 'Octagonal Pond' in an irregular shape. The very fine 'Palladian Bridge' is one of three near-identical bridges built at around the same period; the other two bridges are at Prior Park near Bath (see page 23) and Wilton House near Salisbury.

The parkland became renowned throughout the country and attracted many noble visitors. Brown's first employment at Stowe involved showing visitors around, and in this way probably made many valuable connections that later paid off in the form of commissions to improve the grounds of country houses. Stowe is said to be the first house and grounds for which a guide book was published. The house is, today, home to an English public (fee-paying) school, while the grounds are open to the public through the National Trust.

Left: The building of Stowe House's north front was completed by the 1780s.

PETWORTH HOUSE
AND 'CAPABILITY' BROWN

Lancelot 'Capability' Brown was one of England's leading garden designers when, in 1751, the 2nd Earl of Egremont hired him to redesign the grounds at his 17th-century mansion of Petworth House, West Sussex. Brown created a vast serpentine lake filled via a one-mile (1.6km)-long brick conduit. To do this he moved 47,000 tons of earth and lined the lake with 17,000 tons of clay. He did away with the formal gardens near the house and, by means of skilful plantings of trees, including limes, beeches, sycamores, oaks and horse chestnuts, created the impression that the Earl's parkland led away naturally into the surrounding countryside.

Today, the 700 acre (280 ha) park at Petworth House is celebrated as the finest surviving example of Brown's work. A great herd of fallow deer – the largest and oldest herd in England – graze the park, and come right up to the windows of the house.

'CAPABILITY' BROWN

Born in 1716, Lancelot Brown began life as a gardener's boy in his native Northumberland. His first big break came when he found employment in the gardens at Stowe House in

Buckinghamshire. There he contributed to the creation of one of the country's best-known informal landscape parks, initially working for William Kent but later working as head gardener in his own right.

Following Kent's death in 1748, he set to work independently as a garden designer. He got his nickname of 'Capability' because he was renowned for declaring that places always had 'capabilities of improvement'. In contrast to Kent, he seldom used statuary or classical buildings in his landscaped grounds, preferring to create natural-looking forms using – as at Petworth House – areas of grass, irregularly shaped lakes, the rising and falling of the terrain and trees planted singly and in groups.

Among 'Capability' Brown's many other commissions was his reworking of the park at Blenheim Palace, where he created the splendid lakes that partly submerged John Vanbrugh's majestic bridge. At Chatsworth House, he did away with formal parterres and planted the park, while rerouting the River

Above: More 'natural' than nature. At Petworth House, by moving trees and digging a great lake, 'Capability' Brown created an ideal piece of countryside.

Derwent in a serpentine course more pleasing to the eye. He also worked on the gardens and parks of a great many other prominent country houses, including Audley End, Burghley, Longleat and Syon House.

Below: A neoclassical Doric temple stands in the gardens of Petworth House.

Left: 'Capability' Brown. He learned from the architect and garden designer William Kent.

CHAPTER TWO

LATE GEORGIAN AND REGENCY HOUSES

*c.*1760–1830

In 1811, King George III began rebuilding the state apartments at Windsor Castle in the Gothic style, to the designs of James Wyatt. His reign had seen the rise of Robert Adam and the spread of his 'Adam style' in architecture and interior decoration, which brought a lighter touch, an increased knowledge of 'antique' decoration and a breadth of knowledge of French and Italian influences to the pure Palladianism of the early 18th century.

The Gothic transformation of Windsor Castle was completed by James Wyatt's nephew, Jeffry Wyatville, for George IV. This gradually developing taste for a revival of indigenous English styles in architecture, which can also be seen at Penrhyn Castle in Wales and Dalmeny House in Lothian, Scotland, was partly a reaction to the French Revolution of 1789, forming a desire to set aside continental influences, to emphasize the continuity of British-English traditions and to celebrate great British victories, from Trafalgar to Waterloo.

At around the same time, more exotic influences also made an appearance, as Chinese and 'Hindoo' (Indian-Turkish) styles were enthusiastically employed at Carlton House in London and the Royal Pavilion in Brighton. Then, as the 19th century advanced, these Gothic and Tudor Revivals were balanced by a renewed enthusiasm for classicism in the Greek Revival movement, which was seen in the design of country houses such as Meldon Park, Belsay Hall and The Grange.

Left: In the Great Hall at Syon House, London, the use of recesses and the effect of the black-and-white floor exemplify the 'movement' that was a key element of the 'Adam style'.

STRAWBERRY HILL
AND THE GOTHIC REVIVAL

Writer and connoisseur Horace Walpole, youngest son of Prime Minister Robert Walpole, inspired an architectural movement with his villa at Twickenham, then a country village but now part of south-west London. Over 45 years, beginning in 1747, he added medieval-style towers, battlements, arches, fireplaces, stained-glass windows and other features to transform his villa, Strawberry Hill, beside the River Thames into a 'Gothick Castle'.

The Gothic Revival movement was born in the Georgian era among imitators of Walpole's light-hearted experiments. It then became a more serious and scholarly movement in the 19th century, when it gave rise to buildings such as Sir Charles Barry and A.W.N. Pugin's rebuilt Houses of Parliament at Westminster. The Victorian Gothic Revival continued as a popular style for churches and university buildings well into the 20th century.

Below: The Long Gallery's delicate ceiling at Strawberry Hill was based on that of the Henry VII Chapel in Westminster Abbey.

'COMMITTEE OF TASTE'

Walpole used medieval architectural elements for decorative effect and – because of their romantic associations with little concern for architectural integrity – for reproducing features in the way they would have been used in their original setting. He worked along-side his friends, some of whom he appointed to a 'Committee of Taste', instructed to adapt Gothic architectural details (seen in other buildings or in books of reproductions) for his use at Strawberry Hill. Friends who served on this committee included illustrator

Above: In creating a 'little Gothick Castle' at Strawberry Hill, Walpole indulged his taste for 'charming irregularities' in architecture.

Richard Bentley, John Chute, owner of The Vyne in Hampshire, and poet Thomas Gray.

GOTHIC *SHARAWAGGI*

Walpole chose the Gothic because he was attracted to its lack of symmetry. He was doubtless reacting against the Palladian orthodoxy in England, which called for ordered, harmonious and symmetrical design, and perhaps also

Above: Walpole wrote the first history of art in English, as well as the first Gothic novel.

against the first appearance around him of Neoclassical designs inspired by the temples of ancient Greece. In a letter to his friend Sir Horace Mann, Walpole declared that the trouble with classical-inspired buildings was that they lacked variety and 'charming irregularities'; he was instead attracted, he wrote, to *sharawaggi* or 'want of symmetry'.

Walpole began by 'Gothicizing' the outside of the villa, adding battlements, quatrefoil (four-leaf) windows and Tudor-style chimneys. Subsequently, he built an extension containing a Long Gallery, with a fan-vaulted ceiling based on that of Henry VII's Chapel in Westminster Abbey, and erected two towers – the Beauclerc Tower and the Round Tower.

Strawberry Hill was extended in the mid-19th century by Frances, Countess Waldegrave, who added a new wing. Today the house belongs to St Mary's College, part of the University of Surrey.

Besides building Strawberry Hill and leaving a vast collection of letters that provide a wonderful picture of 18th-century aristocratic life, Walpole's other claim to fame is that he was the author of the first 'Gothic novel'. His *The Castle of Otranto* was first published anonymously in 1765, supposedly as a translation of an Italian book of 1529. Earlier in 1757, he had established a

private press at Strawberry Hill, in which he published several of his own books and Thomas Gray's *Odes*.

THE VYNE

In 1754, Walpole's friend John Chute inherited The Vyne in Hampshire – a Tudor mansion later given the first classical portico on an English country house. A member of Walpole's 'Committee of Taste' – which often met in The Vyne – Chute shared his friend's passion for the 'Gothic'; Walpole referred to him as 'my oracle in taste …

Above: Walpole's reinvention of the Gothic has had a wide influence. Strawberry Hill does not look as unusual today as it did when new.

the genius that presided over poor Strawberry!' Chute intended to Gothicize the entire interior of The Vyne (indeed, he had his portrait painted while holding a plan for a Gothicized interior at the house) but, in the event, applied the new style only to one room, the Ante-chapel. Elsewhere, he used a serene classical style to build a staircase and galleries in place of the Tudor Great Hall.

ARBURY HALL, WARWICKSHIRE

Sir Roger Newdigate, for 30 years from 1750 MP for Oxford University, was a pioneer of the Georgian Gothic Revival in his house at Arbury, Warwickshire. His exuberant and light-hearted alterations of an old house of monastic origins were, like those at Strawberry Hill, chiefly for decorative effect, having no structural function. In the Drawing Room (designed in 1762), he installed a fireplace inspired by the tomb of Aymer de Valence in Westminster Abbey. The Dining Room (designed by Henry Keene *c.*1772) has an elaborate fan vault and another extraordinary chimney-piece. The Saloon

(designed by Henry Couchman and Sir Roger in 1776–96) is probably the house's finest room and features delicate plaster tracery above its large bow window. The novelist, George Eliot, grew up on the estate and represented Sir Roger and his house in her *Scenes of Clerical Life* (1858). Sir Roger is also remembered as the founder of the Newdigate Poetry Prize for Oxford University students, won by poets such as Matthew Arnold and Andrew Motion.

Right: An extravaganza of delicate and beautifully finished plasterwork rises above the bow window in the Arbury Hall Saloon.

KEW PALACE
AND QUEEN CHARLOTTE'S COTTAGE

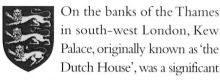 On the banks of the Thames in south-west London, Kew Palace, originally known as 'the Dutch House', was a significant royal residence between 1728 and 1818. Apart from Queen Charlotte's Cottage, the orangery and pagoda, the palace is the only surviving royal building of many that once stood at Kew.

Kew Palace is a fairly modest four-storey brick manor house, built in 1631 by Dutch merchant, Samuel Fortrey: his initials, those of his wife, and the date can be seen on a carved brick set above the south door. It is a villa, with symmetrical south and north façades featuring pediments and pilasters. Its chief room is the King's Dining Room, measuring 31 x 21ft (9.3 x 6.3m), with ceiling decoration featuring a Tudor rose.

The house was leased by Queen Caroline in 1728; William Kent added new stairs and sash windows at this time. It was principally used as a residence for the princesses Anne, Amelia and Caroline. Then, in the 1750s, Frederick, Prince of Wales, was

Below: This engraving shows Kew Palace as it was c. 1815–20, around the time when Queen Charlotte lived there briefly.

living in the adjacent White House and used the Dutch House as a school for his eldest sons, George, Prince of Wales (the future George III), and Prince Edward. The house was again a princely school in the 1770s, this time for George III's sons George, Prince of Wales, and Frederick, Duke of York.

King George bought the house outright in 1781. In 1801–6, he lived there occasionally with Queen Charlotte; by this stage the King's health was poor following recurrent attacks of porphyria. He subsequently lived mainly at Windsor. Then Queen Charlotte, herself seriously ill, lived in Kew Palace for the

Above: Palace and formal garden. After a major restoration by Historic Royal Palaces, Kew Palace opened to the public in April 2006.

last few months of her life in 1818 – during which three royal weddings took place in the building. These were the marriages of Prince Adolphus to Princess Augusta of Hesse-Cassel, of William, Duke of Clarence (the future William IV), to Princess Adelaide of Saxe-Meiningen and of Edward, Duke of Kent, to Princess Victoire of Saxe-Coburg (the parents of Queen Victoria).

THE WHITE HOUSE, KEW

Kew Palace originally stood alongside a much larger royal residence: Kew House. This was used by George III's parents, Frederick, Prince of Wales, and his wife, Princess Augusta, from the 1730s onward. It was rebuilt by William Kent, who gave it a coolly elegant white stucco façade that earned the building its new name of 'the White House'. Kent also designed the lavish interiors.

Frederick died in 1751 and Augusta lived on in the White House as Dowager Princess of Wales. Several buildings and features in the gardens were built for her by Sir William Chambers, including an orangery and pagoda. The house was demolished in the early 19th century.

Right: White Lodge, Richmond Park. George II's queen, Caroline, loved this Palladian villa. The future Edward VIII was born here on 23 June 1894.

RICHMOND LODGE

Another riverside residence with delightful gardens was Richmond Lodge in Richmond Old Deer Park. It stood on the site of a ruined ancient royal palace, in a position where Charles II had considered building a new residence to designs by Sir Christopher Wren; William III subsequently built a hunting lodge on the ancient ruins. The future George II and Queen Caroline used William III's lodge as Prince and Princess of Wales from 1718 and, after coming to the throne, made it Queen Caroline's dower house. In the 1730s, Charles Bridgeman and William Kent redesigned the gardens, adding a temple, a dairy and even a 'Merlin's Cave'. (These grounds and those surrounding the Dutch House and the White House were joined together during George III's reign and became the Royal Botanic Gardens of Kew in 1841.)

George III and Queen Charlotte used Richmond Lodge as a country house for over a decade after 1761, but in 1772 they moved into the White House, following the death of his mother, and the lodge was demolished.

THE 'NEW PALACE'

King George III had grand plans for a new palace in the Old Deer Park, Richmond. Sir William Chambers drew up three sets of plans, the first of which was for a Palladian-style palace with a Corinthian portico like that of Holkham Hall, but these all came to nothing. Then, in 1800, James Wyatt designed a Gothic-style castle-palace with a square central keep and four cylindrical towers. Building began in 1801 on the site of the demolished White House and continued for a decade at a cost of £500,000. But work was halted in 1811 because of the King's illness, at a stage when the castle was just a shell. George IV hated the new palace and had it destroyed with explosives in 1827.

THE WHITE LODGE

The New Park Lodge (or White Lodge) in Richmond Park was a hunting lodge in the form of a Palladian villa, designed by Roger Morris for George I in 1727. This building stands in the park we know today as Richmond Park, which was originally called the New Park. (The New Park is on the other side of Richmond from the older royal hunting grounds of the Old Deer Park.) George died before the lodge was finished and George II completed it for Queen Caroline. Today it is the junior section of the Royal Ballet School.

Below: William Chambers drew inspiration from a youthful visit to China when he designed the 163ft (50m)- tall Great Pagoda for the Dowager Princess Augusta in 1761.

THE QUEEN'S COTTAGE

Queen Charlotte's Cottage stands in a nature conservation area amid a wild bluebell wood in Kew Gardens. The cottage was given to Queen Charlotte, in September 1761, on her marriage to George III. The royals used the building as a summerhouse. In 1818 it was the venue for the tea, following the double wedding of her sons William, Duke of Clarence, and Edward, Duke of Kent.

Below: Queen Charlotte's Cottage was opened to visitors in 1959.

SYON HOUSE
AND ROBERT ADAM

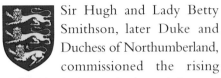

Sir Hugh and Lady Betty Smithson, later Duke and Duchess of Northumberland, commissioned the rising architect-designer Robert Adam to remodel and redecorate the interior of Syon House, Middlesex, in 1762. The house, built in the mid-16th century by Edward Seymour, Duke of Somerset and Lord Protector of the Kingdom, already had a long and colourful history.

Adam was forced to work with the structure he inherited, for Sir Hugh and Lady Betty did not want him to rebuild the Tudor mansion and turned down his request to build a circular domed room in the central courtyard. Instead, he created a suite of five rooms running around the west, south and east sides of the courtyard house.

THE 'ADAM STYLE'

Adam's five rooms – the Great Hall, the Ante-room, the Dining Room, the Red Drawing Room and the Long Gallery

Below: The Red Drawing Room. The finest Spitalfields silk hangs on its walls.

– lead one into another. They are celebrated as the first fully realized statement of the 'Adam style', which deployed ancient Roman architectural elements with a new freedom and lightness of touch. The key element of the 'Adam style' is 'movement', which Robert and James defined in the Preface to *The Works in Architecture of Robert and James Adam* (two volumes, 1773 and 1779) as 'the rise and fall, the advance and recess, with other diversity of form, in the different parts of a building'.

Adam's use of recesses and steps in the cool black-and-white Great Hall at Syon House exemplifies this movement. In the gorgeously grand Ante-room he brought Rome to London in the form of a dozen green antique marble columns found on the bed of the River Tiber. The floor of muted yellow, red and blue makes a harmonious composition with the gold of the statues on top of the columns and the gilt stucco panels in the walls.

'GREAT VARIETY'

The Dining Room, a triple cube 63ft long by 21ft wide and high (19 x 6 x 6m), contains gilt and ivory decoration. The Red Drawing Room has sumptuous red silk wall coverings, an elegant coved ceiling beautifully painted by Angelica Kauffman and a fine carpet designed by Adam and woven by Thomas Moore in 1769. After this series of triumphs, Adam achieved perhaps his finest effect in redecorating the Jacobean-era Long Gallery. This room, 136ft long by 14ft wide and high (41 x 4 x 4m), was decorated and furnished in a colour scheme of pale green and gilt, with bookshelves and furniture of his own design. He achieved, in his own words, 'a style to afford great variety and amusement'.

Right: These designs, including folding doors, are from one of Adam's pattern books.

Above: Grandly transformed within, thanks to its Adam decorations, on the outside Syon House is a rather plain Tudor block.

AMERICAN CONNECTION

Robert Adam's patron at Syon House, Sir Hugh Smithson, had an illegitimate son named James Smithson, born in France to his mistress, Elizabeth Kate Hungerford Macie. James was a chemist and geologist, and on his death in 1829 he left $508,318 to found 'an establishment for the increase and diffusion of knowledge among men': the result was the Smithsonian Institution, established in Washington, D.C., in 1846.

HAREWOOD HOUSE
AND THE 'ADAM STYLE'

The stately Palladian mansion of Harewood House, near Leeds, was built in 1759–72 for the immensely wealthy Edwin Lascelles, 1st Lord Harewood. John Carr of York designed the main block, while Robert Adam was responsible for the side wings and interiors.

CHIPPENDALE AND ADAM

The 16 staterooms on the principal floor of the house are exquisitely decorated and furnished in the 'Adam style', with elegant chairs and other furniture by the leading 18th-century cabinetmaker Thomas Chippendale. Adam's grand Entrance Hall has Doric half-columns painted to imitate red marble; they make a telling contrast with the elegant grey-blue walls. The room now called the China Room was originally the Study in Adam's plan; it contains a collection of superb Sèvres porcelain with pieces once owned by Louis XV and XVI and Queen Marie Antoinette.

The State Bedroom was intended for visiting members of the royal family: it contains magnificent Chippendale pieces including a spectacular state bed, fine wall mirrors and a satinwood commode and secretaire that many identify as Chippendale's finest work. The less

Above: Originally, Harewood House's south front gave on to the park, but a formal terrace garden was added in the mid-19th century.

grand East Bedroom was used by 1st Lord Harewood: it retains its Adam frieze and sunflower ceiling decoration.

The sumptuous Long Gallery is 77ft long, 24ft wide and 21ft high (23 x 7 x 6m). The ceiling was designed by Adam and painted by Biagio Rebecca. Of all the staterooms, the Music Room remains closest to Adam's original design: the colourful Adam carpet contains lyres and reflects the ceiling roundels painted by Angelica Kauffman; trumpets, lyres and pipes are carved in the marble chimney-piece; the chairs and sofas, and even the frame for the portrait of the 1st Earl's sister-in-law are by Chippendale.

LATER ALTERATIONS

In 1772, Lancelot 'Capability' Brown began to redesign the park. In the 19th century, Sir Charles Barry removed Carr's classical portico on the south front, added a third storey to the house and swept away part of Brown's landscape to create a terrace garden. For part of the 20th century, Harewood House was home to George V's daughter, Mary, the Princess Royal, who married the 6th Earl of Harewood in 1922. The house, today, belongs to her son George, the 7th Earl, who is the Queen's first cousin.

ROBERT ADAM

The architect and designer Robert Adam was born in 1728 in Fife, son of the leading Scottish architect of his day, William Adam, who served as Master Mason to the North British Board of Ordnance. On his father's death in 1748, Robert and his brother James were appointed to the position and in 1748–54 undertook many architectural and decorating commissions, including Fort George, near Inverness, and Dumfries House in Ayrshire. After travelling in continental Europe in 1754–7, Robert settled in London and soon made his name with his 'Adam style'.

By 1761 he was already receiving major commissions to redecorate the interiors of grand houses both in London and in the country, such as Alnwick Castle (Northumberland), Kedleston Hall (Derbyshire) and Osterley Park (Middlesex – now the London Borough of Hounslow). In the same year he was appointed Architect to the King's Works. Both before and after his work on the interior at Syon House in 1762, Adam was architect on a number of houses, designing the south front at Kedleston Hall in 1757–9, then building Mersham-le-Hatch (Kent) in 1762–72 and Luton Hoo (Bedfordshire) in 1766–74; he remodelled Kenwood House in 1767–8. In later life he designed a number of Gothic Revival castles including Culzean in Ayrshire; he is particularly remembered in Scotland for his design of Edinburgh University and of Edinburgh's Charlotte Square. He died in 1792 and was buried in Westminster Abbey.

Left: Robert Adam closely studied the architecture of ancient Greece and Rome to create the 'Adam style'.

KEDLESTON HALL
AND KENWOOD HOUSE

 Robert Adam was initially commissioned at Kedleston Hall *c.*1758 to design classical temples and rustic buildings in the park, while Sir Nathaniel Curzon, subsequently 1st Baron Scarsdale, was rebuilding his family mansion. But Adam impressed Sir Nathaniel sufficiently to be granted control over the design of the house, ousting architects Matthew Brettingham and James Paine.

DRAMATIC FAÇADE

Adam's south front contains a four-column triumphal arch – based on the Arch of Constantine in Rome – beneath a domed roof and above a beautiful curving double staircase, which leads up to a large glass entrance door. To right and left of this central block are identical wings of three floors. The façade combines great drama with wonderful delicacy, and – perfectly embodying the Adam concept of 'movement' – is considered both a quintessential Robert Adam design and an architectural masterpiece.

Below: The Marble Hall at Kedleston, with its 20 pink alabaster columns, lies directly behind the vast portico on the north front.

Kedleston was the first building to make use of a triumphal arch in an English stately house.

The impressive north, or entrance, front, 350ft (107m) across, was beg un by Brettingham. It consists of two substantial end pavilions linked to the main block by curving corridors. The east pavilion contains rooms for the use of Sir Nathaniel and family, the main block houses the staterooms and the west pavilion the service quarters. The main building has an imposing six-column

Above: The north front at Kedleston was largely as designed by Brettingham, but Adam emphasised the six-column portico.

portico; it was begun by Paine and completed by Adam in more dramatic style than originally planned.

MARBLE AND ALABASTER

The portico entrance leads into the grandly classical Great Hall, probably designed by Brettingham like a Roman basilica, along the lines of the equally magnificent Marble Hall he built with William Kent and Lord Leicester at Holkham Hall, Norfolk.

The Great Hall at Kedleston has an Italian marble floor and contains 20 fluted alabaster columns set before alcoves containing classical statues; the walls and doors are decorated with classical scenes; the hall fills the entire height of the house and the only sources of light are the skylights in the roof. The hall leads into the circular Saloon, which stands behind the arch of the south front and is lit from above through glass in the dome 62ft (19m) above. The room was designed as a sculpture gallery; it contains four sets of double doors, with surrounds of green *scagliola*.

KEDLESTON AND INDIA

Kedleston Hall was the model for the residence of the Governor-General of India, the Raj Bhavan in Calcutta, which was built in 1799–1803, complete with Palladian columns and dome. The Raj Bhavan was later occupied by Lord Curzon, Viceroy of India in 1898–1905, who must have enjoyed the familiarity of the surroundings because, as a descendant of Sir Nathaniel Curzon, he had been born at Kedleston Hall in 1859. Kedleston Hall has an 'Indian museum' containing artefacts and furniture brought back to Derbyshire by Lord Curzon; the former Viceroy's tomb stands in the tiny 13th-century church in the grounds at Kedleston – the only remnant of the medieval village that was moved during the creation of the 18th-century landscape park.

The other staterooms include the Great Apartment – a formal bedroom with gilded chairs and a superb state bed – and the Drawing Room, which boasts a chimney-piece of the Derbyshire stone bluejohn and doorcases and window surrounds made from local alabaster. The other main rooms are the Dining Room, the Library and the Music Room. A magnificent staircase leads down from the principal rooms on the *piano nobile* to Caesar's Hall on the ground floor.

ADAM'S LANDSCAPED PARK

At Kedleston Hall, Adam also landscaped the 820-acre (332-ha) park with the help of the landscape gardener, William Emes. He created five serpentine lakes in the style of 'Capability' Brown from canals and ponds that had been laid out earlier by Charles Bridgeman. Adam also built a beautifully judged bridge, fishing house and boat house, as well as a number of classical buildings, such as the North Lodge – which was another triumphal arch.

KENWOOD HOUSE

In 1764–79, Robert Adam remodelled the early 17th-century Kenwood House in Hampstead for the Scottish-born politician and judge, William Murray, 1st Earl of Mansfield. Adam built an Ionic portico on the north, or entrance, front and created a celebrated library on the east side of the south front. The Library's widely admired interior has a curved ceiling with flat oval and rectangular panels for decoration, its shape described by Adam as 'much more perfect than that which is commonly called the cove ceiling'. The house originally stood close to the road from Hampstead to Highgate, but in the 1790s the 2nd Earl of Mansfield moved the road; the house now stands in a secluded position on Hampstead Heath, in gardens designed by Humphry Repton. The 1999 film *Notting Hill* was partly filmed at Kenwood House.

IVEAGH BEQUEST

In 1928, Kenwood House and a substantial collection of fine art was bequeathed to the nation by Edward Cecil Guinness, the 1st Earl of Iveagh, head of the Guinness brewing family from Ireland and the man responsible for the lavish rebuilding of Elveden Hall in Suffolk. Lord Iveagh built up the art collection in the late 19th century. It included some very important

Above: The highly colourful Library at Kenwood House is thought to be one of the finest of all Robert Adam interiors.

paintings, including a self-portrait of *c.*1665 by Rembrandt, the delicate *Guitar Player* by Vermeer and several fine works by Turner, Lawrence and Reynolds. Further paintings have been added to The Iveagh Bequest over the years. They are on display in the beautiful surroundings of Kenwood House.

Below: A modern touch at Kedleston Hall. In the recesses of the Saloon, the pedestals beneath the urns are actually stoves.

HEVENINGHAM HALL
AND JAMES WYATT

When James Wyatt returned to London from six years' study in Italy in 1768, he quickly won national renown for his theatre, The Pantheon, in Regent Street. The extraordinary domed building, which opened in 1772 but was later demolished, was based on the design of the Hagia Sophia ('Church of Sacred Wisdom') in Istanbul. Horace Walpole called it 'the most beautiful edifice in England'.

Wyatt began to work as a country-house architect in the Neoclassical style at Heaton Hall in Lancashire (1772); at Heveningham Hall, Suffolk, the Dutch merchant Sir Gerard Vanneck commissioned him in 1788 to complete the grand 25-bay remodelling (begun by Sir Robert Taylor) of an earlier house.

Wyatt was principally responsible for Heveningham Hall's interiors, which include the beautiful Vaulted Hall. The rooms are considered to be among Wyatt's finest work and have recently been restored and renovated.

Heveningham Hall still stands in extensive parkland, which was originally set out by Lancelot 'Capability' Brown. This includes a stable block in the shape of a horseshoe, a temple and an ice-house. The recent restoration includes the addition of further Neoclassical

Above: The great expanse of Heveningham Hall. Between them, Wyatt and Taylor created a most impressive house.

buildings, including a bridge across the lake, a new temple, an orangery and a boat house.

Below: Inner beauty. Heveningham Hall – detail of James Wyatt's library.

JAMES WYATT

Born in 1746 in Staffordshire, James Wyatt was still in his twenties when he set out as a country-house architect with his work at Heaton Hall. He became Robert Adam's great rival in the Neoclassical style, but could work with equal success in the Gothic Revival mode. Wyatt enjoyed a long career that stretched into the second decade of the 19th century; from 1796 he served as Surveyor General to the Board of Works and was involved in the restoration of many great English cathedrals, including Durham, Salisbury and Hereford. His ventures into the Gothic were dismissed by more serious followers of the Gothic Revival in the mid-19th century. Wyatt built a number of Gothic Revival country houses, including Lee Priory in Kent

(1783–90) and Ashridge in Hertfordshire (1808 onward). But he is remembered, above all, as the designer of the extravagant and extraordinary Gothic country house of Fonthill Abbey in Wiltshire (now ruined), built in 1796–1807 for William Beckford, author of *Vathek* (1786).

Below: The design for Fonthill Abbey. Its steepled tower collapsed three times.

CASTLE COOLE
AND THE NEOCLASSICAL REVIVAL

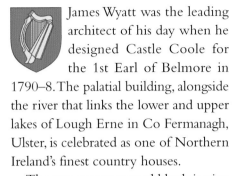

James Wyatt was the leading architect of his day when he designed Castle Coole for the 1st Earl of Belmore in 1790–8. The palatial building, alongside the river that links the lower and upper lakes of Lough Erne in Co Fermanagh, Ulster, is celebrated as one of Northern Ireland's finest country houses.

The two-storey central block is nine bays in width. On the entrance front, a towering pedimented portico containing four plain Ionic columns 27ft (8m) tall stands in the centre of the main block; on either side, two wings each fronted by a colonnade of six Doric columns lead to an end pavilion. On the garden front, the central bow is curved on account of the Oval Saloon within. Wyatt used pale Portland stone brought at great expense from Dorset. The stone was taken by ship to Ballyshannon (Co Donegal), carried overland to Lough Erne, then shipped by barge across the water as far as Enniskillen, before being brought the final 2 miles (3km) by cart.

Below: The entrance hall, Castle Coole. The door leads to the Oval Saloon.

TOP-LIT LOBBY

Behind the entrance portico, the restrained Great Hall is of one storey only and contains a line of Doric columns, two plain chimney-pieces and a Doric frieze. The hall gives on to the Staircase Hall, which contains a double-return stone staircase up to a first-floor landing with four Doric columns of brown and yellow *scagliola*. The lobby, also on the first floor, is lit from above, in line with Irish country-house tradition, by glass domes hidden on the entrance front behind pediment and balustrade. The lobby contains an attic-level gallery, from which rooms lead off,

Above: The main front at Castle Coole. Note the elegant symmetry of the two Doric colonnades leading to twin end pavilions.

with a graceful colonnade said to be copied from the interiors of the temple of the sea god Poseidon at Paestum and the Parthenon in Athens.

Behind the curved centre of the garden front is the elegant Oval Saloon, which runs out to the Drawing Room and Dining Room on either side, with plasterwork to Wyatt's designs by Joseph Rose of London and *scagliola* work by Dominic Bartoli.

THE GREEK REVIVAL

In his use of more austere, less ornamented ancient Greek rather than Roman architectural elements, for example the baseless column used in the colonnades on the entrance front, Wyatt followed the fashion for Hellenism in Neoclassical architecture at the close of the century. Under the influence of James Stuart and Nicholas Revett's *The Antiquities of Athens* (published in three parts in 1762, 1789 and 1795), a growing interest in archaeology and the discovery of Greek antiquities, Neoclassicists held that ancient Greek architecture was purer and more rational than ancient Roman building. This enthusiasm fed into the Greek Revival movement of the 19th century.

ALTHORP
THE SPENCERS AND THE ROYALS

In *c.*1790 Henry Holland handsomely refaced the Spencer family's country house at Althorp, Northamptonshire, also adding pediments to the south and north fronts and corridors along the forecourt wings. By this date the Spencers were already well established at Althorp, having lived there since 1508, when Sir John Spencer bought the original moated medieval manor house, built of a local orange stone, with grounds of 300 acres (120ha). Today, Althorp is one of the most visited country houses in England,

Above: Classical good taste. Althorp is an Elizabethan house in 18th-century dress.

for its estate contains the burial place of Diana, Princess of Wales, whose father was the 8th Earl Spencer.

THE GROWTH OF ALTHORP
The first Sir John Spencer or his grandson, another Sir John, rebuilt the medieval house at Althorp to make a more substantial redbrick dwelling with an internal courtyard. Then, in 1575, the younger Sir John added two wings on the south side to create the entrance forecourt. In 1660–2, Dorothy, widow of Henry Spencer, 1st Earl of Sunderland, covered the internal courtyard and built the Grand Staircase. Her son, Robert Spencer, 2nd Earl of Sunderland, created a classical façade with columns and balustrade, and internally transformed the Great Hall on the upper floor of the west wing into a Long Gallery, while on the north side creating staterooms including the Saloon. He had formal gardens laid out to designs by the Frenchman André Le Nôtre, landscaper of the royal Palace of Versailles. The house in this era greatly impressed diarist John Evelyn, who called it a 'palace…a noble pile',

PRINCESS DIANA AND ALTHORP
Lady Diana Spencer was born at Park House on the Sandringham estate. Her parents divorced in 1969, when she was eight, and her father was awarded custody of the children. He inherited Althorp in 1975 when she was 13, and she spent her teenage years there, when she was not at boarding school or staying at her mother's home in London. Indeed, she first met her future husband, Prince Charles, at Althorp when he visited to shoot in November 1977.

Following her death in Paris in 1997, her body was brought in a cortege from the funeral at Westminster Abbey to Althorp, where she was interred on an island in the lake known as the Round Oval. An urn on the island, designed by Edward Bulmer and made by Dick Reid, celebrates her memory, which is also honoured by an exhibition of her life and work in Althorp's Italianate stables, built by Roger Morris *c.*1733. The summerhouse by the lake is set aside in her memory.

Below: The summerhouse at Althorp, now a memorial to Diana, once stood in the grounds of Admiralty House, London.

Below: Princess Diana in May 1997. As Lady Diana Spencer, she spent part of her childhood at Althorp.

and declared its rooms and furnishings to be 'such as may become a great prince', also noting that its gardens were both 'exquisitely planted and kept'.

The next stage of work was in the 18th century. First, Charles Spencer, the 5th Earl of Sunderland, refashioned the Entrance Hall following Palladian designs by Colen Campbell that were actually implemented by Roger Morris after Campbell's death (1729); Morris also built the stone stables with two classical porticoes, and artist John Wootton painted a series of Spencer hunting scenes. Then, George Spencer, the 2nd Earl Spencer, commissioned the fashionable architect Henry Holland – who was simultaneously working for the Prince of Wales on the Marine Pavilion in Brighton (later rebuilt as Brighton Pavilion) and redesigning Carlton House in London – literally to give the essentially Elizabethan house an 18th-century facelift.

A 'MATHEMATICAL' FAÇADE

Holland refaced the red brick with white brick rebate tiles, which were called 'mathematical tiles' by contemporaries because they fitted together so exactly. The view then current was that brick was not a suitable material for a

grand house, despite the great and enduring beauty of Tudor brick houses such as Compton Wynyates; rebate tiles were popularized by Holland, who used them to face his own London house, Sloane Place.

In addition to adding pediments to the garden and entrance fronts, Holland filled in the medieval moat, and within the house moved the main reception rooms to the ground floor of the west wing, creating a fine progression of

Above: At Althorp, Earl Spencer stands before a 1994 portrait of Diana that once hung in her home, Kensington Palace.

rooms through the Long Library, the Yellow Drawing Room and the Dining Room. Althorp has changed little over the 200-odd years since Holland's alterations were carried out: although a medieval and Elizabethan house at its core, its classical 18th-century facing dominates its appearance and gives it its essential character.

THE SPENCER 'FAMILY SILVER'

Althorp is also celebrated for the Spencer family's superb collection of sculpture, ceramics, furniture and paintings, including fine works by Rubens, van Dyck, Lely, Reynolds and Gainsborough. In addition, it contains widely admired doors, chimney-pieces and other fittings designed by John Vardy and James 'Athenian' Stuart for the family's London mansion, Spencer House, in the 18th century. The fittings were removed to Althorp when Spencer House was leased in 1924.

Left: Althorp is full of the finest furniture, paintings and other fittings – much of it brought there from Spencer House, London.

BRIGHTON PAVILION
AND THE PRINCE REGENT

The exotic domes and minarets of the Royal Pavilion in Brighton were built in 1815–23 by architect John Nash for George, the former Prince of Wales, who was Prince Regent in 1811–20 due to the illness of his father, George III, and King in 1820–30. Nash used the briefly fashionable 'Hindoo' style, derived mainly from that of Islamic temple architecture in India and a strain of the taste for the exotic that flowered in the Regency period, partly in reaction to the uncluttered, 'rational' designs of Palladian and Neoclassical architects. Nash built on and around the Prince's earlier house, the Marine Pavilion, which had itself been constructed on the site of a humble farmhouse by Henry Holland from 1787 onward.

Above: Oriental romance by the Sussex sea – the domes and minarets of the Pavilion suggest a temple more than a palace.

GEORGE'S FIRST PAVILION

George, Prince of Wales, was very taken with Brighton – then a village called Brighthelmstone – when he first visited in 1783 to stay with his uncle, the Duke of Cumberland. George returned in 1784 and leased a farmhouse on the Steine, an area of grassy land to the east of the village, later setting up home there with his Roman Catholic wife, Maria Fitzherbert, whom he had secretly married in 1785. The house built on this site by Henry Holland was Neoclassical, with a domed saloon and wings extending to south and north.

In 1802–3, the Prince began to redevelop his Pavilion in an oriental style. Initially, the look was Chinese rather than 'Hindoo': he redecorated the interior of the house with bamboo panelling and with Chinese chimney-pieces, wallpaper, porcelain, statuary and furniture, and commissioned William Porden to refashion the exterior as a Chinese pagoda. But then the Prince's taste turned to Indian- and Turkish-inspired architecture, and in 1804–8 he had Porden build a splendid domed stable block and riding school in a 'Saracenic' style that most closely resembles a Turkish mosque.

NASH REPLACES REPTON

The prominent landscape gardener, Humphry Repton, was known to the Prince because he had worked on the gardens at Carlton House in London. He was invited to Brighton, where he acclaimed Porden's domed stable block as 'stupendous and magnificent…distinct from either Grecian or Gothic' and drew up a detailed plan to rebuild the entire Pavilion in a 'Hindoo' style. The Prince declared himself delighted and indicated that he would 'have every part

Left: The Court at Brighton à la *Chinese. Cruikshank's cartoon satirizes George's lavishly indulged taste for the Oriental.*

Above: It cost more than £500,000 to furnish the Banqueting Room, a setting for exotic dinners, in such brilliant luxury.

JOHN NASH

After training under Sir Robert Taylor, Nash began his career as a speculative builder in London. Declared bankrupt in 1783, he moved into country-house architecture to rebuild his reputation and worked with landscape gardener Humphry Repton. Nash returned to London in the 1790s and from 1798 was employed by the Prince of Wales, later working on redesigning the Brighton Pavilion and the rebuilding of Buckingham House in London, as well as developing Regent's Park and Regent's Street. Nash's own house, East Cowes Castle on the Isle of Wight, was an influence on the early 19th-century phase of the Gothic Revival. His country houses include the 'picturesque' Italianate Cronkhill in Shropshire (1802) and Sandridge Park in Devon (*c.*1805), and also the Gothic Revival-style Caerhays Castle in Cornwall (1808). He also built four Gothic castles in Ireland, including Killymoon Castle in County Tyrone (1803).

of it carried into immediate execution'. Due to financial difficulties, however, he did not actually begin the work until 1815, and then, to Repton's dismay, it was carried out to designs by John Nash.

Using a cast-iron framework over Holland's original house, Nash added the distinctive onion-shaped domes, minarets, cupolas and pinnacles that give the Pavilion such a distinctive look today. The interior was lavish, decorated and furnished with great Regency wit and an extravagant sense of the exotic. First, Nash built a new pink and green Entrance Hall and light green Long Gallery, decorated in the Chinese style with dragon panels. Then he planned the kitchen with four remarkable iron columns, made to look like palm trees with bronze leaves, to support the lantern roof, and equipped it with all the latest gadgets to enable the staff to get food to the Prince Regent's table piping hot.

PUBLIC ROOMS

Next, in 1812–20, he built new end wings containing the Pavilion's main apartments, the Music Room and the Banqueting Room, each measuring 40 x 60ft (12 x 18m). In the Banqueting Room, the 45ft (13.5m)- high domed ceiling was painted to resemble an eastern sky with a silver dragon holding a vast chandelier, lit by gas rather than candles, and almost a ton in weight and 30ft (9m) high. The Music Room also had a domed ceiling and gas chandelier; here, the Prince entertained his guests with music performed by an orchestra dressed in Turkish costumes, sometimes himself singing as a baritone. On one occasion, he received the Italian composer Gioacchino Rossini there. In his private apartments, George had a bath 6ft deep, 10ft wide and 16ft long (1.2 x 3 x 4.8m), which was filled with salt water pumped directly from the sea.

AN ABANDONED PALACE

George apparently grew bored of all this splendour: after 1827 he did not return to the Pavilion, preferring Windsor Castle and Buckingham Palace. As Brighton grew, so the Pavilion was gradually surrounded by housing and the King felt the need for greater privacy. According to some accounts, he finally abandoned his Brighton house because his new mistress, Lady Conyngham, declared that she disliked it. Among his successors, William IV used the Pavilion, but Queen Victoria loathed it and was considering having it knocked down before she and Albert settled at Osborne. The building, owned by the Brighton local authority, has recently been restored.

Below: This contemporary aquatint indicates that the Pavilion may simply have been too grand for comfortable living.

PENRHYN CASTLE
AND THE NORMAN REVIVAL

The favoured royal architect, Thomas Hopper, built the Norman-style Penrhyn Castle near Bangor *c*.1825. This romantic building, complete with turrets and battlements, was one of a series of early 19th-century houses in the shape of Norman and Tudor castles – in what came to be known as the Norman and Tudor Revival styles.

Before building Penrhyn Castle, Hopper served the Prince of Wales by designing a glass-and-iron 'Gothick' conservatory at the Prince's lavish town-house, Carlton House, in 1807. In 1819 he began Gosford Castle in Co Armagh, Northern Ireland, for Archibald Acheson, 2nd Earl of Gosford, who later served as Governor of Canada. Built of pale local Bessbrook granite with an angular keep, circular towers and bastions, Gosford was Ireland's largest country house when built.

Hopper's patrons at Penrhyn were the relations of a Liverpool merchant, Richard Pennant, who had built up a great fortune from Jamaican sugar and, after 1785, developed the local Penrhyn Quarry for mining slate. The castle at

Below: 'Prodigy house' revisited. Anthony Salvin's extravagant Harlaxton Hall used a hybrid Elizabethan-Jacobean Revival style.

Penrhyn incorporates a medieval hall dating to the time of Llywelyn ap Iorwerth ('Llywelyn the Great') and a later 'mock castle'. Hopper designed the castle interior and fittings using fine wallpapers, 'Norman' furniture, stained glass and delicate carvings. The building and fitting took 25 years (1820–45).

Penrhyn Castle also contains a splendid Grand Staircase, a bed made of local slate weighing one ton for a visit by Queen Victoria, and a magnificent art collection put together by the Pennant family. Its kitchens and servant quarters have

Above: Penrhyn Castle stands in 45 acres (18ha) of park. In spring, the daffodils and snowdrops are a glorious sight, with distant views of Snowdonia to further stir the spirit.

been restored to their condition in 1894, when they were prepared for a banquet in honour of a visit by the Prince of Wales (the future Edward VII). With magnificent views of Snowdonia and the Menai Straits, the castle stands in impressive grounds, which include a sheltered walled garden with many tropical plants such as palm trees and Chinese gooseberries.

REVIVAL STYLES

At the close of the 18th century and in the early 19th century, architectural styles for country houses became increasingly diverse. The general adherence to Palladian and Neoclassical designs was submerged in a return to a number of earlier styles, including the Gothic, Tudor (sometimes called Elizabethan), Jacobean and Greek Revivals.

THREE REVIVAL CASTLES

A precursor of the Norman Revival was the castellated Norris Castle on the Isle of Wight, built on the site of a 16th-century fortress by James Wyatt for Lord Henry Seymour in the 1790s. (Happy memories of childhood visits here led Queen Victoria to buy Osborne nearby.)

In 1810–20, Sir Robert Smirke then used the Norman Revival style at Eastnor Castle in the Malvern Hills for John Somers Cocks, the 1st Earl Somers. Within the castle, Sir George Gilbert Scott built a Great Hall measuring 55ft high, 30ft wide and 60ft long (17 x 9 x 18m) and A.M.W. Pugin used the Gothic Revival style in the Drawing Room.

In Northern Ireland, Edward Blore employed the Tudor Revival style – sometimes called 'Tudor-Gothic' or 'Elizabethan Revival' – at Narrow Water Castle in Co Down in the 1830s. His patron was Roger Hall, High Sheriff of Co Down. The elegant Revival house stands alongside a long house built in a loose Wren style in the 17th century and close to the original 13th-century Norman castle on the site. Blore's castle has a beautiful interior with exquisite panelling, plasterwork, wooden over-mantel and furniture.

OTHER REVIVAL BUILDINGS

A similar Tudor Revival style was used by the architect William Wilkins in 1815 for Dalmeny House in Lothian, Scotland, and the following year for his reworking of Tregothnan, near Truro, in Cornwall. Both have the elaborate profile of an Elizabethan 'prodigy house'. Jeffry Wyatville used Tudor

Revival elements at Lilleshall Hall in Shropshire in the 1820s–30s for George Granville Leveson-Gower, Marquis of Stafford and later 1st Duke of Sutherland. Around the same time William Burn built an Elizabethan Revival mansion, Carstairs House, Strathclyde, for Henry Montieth.

The extraordinary Harlaxton Hall at Harlaxton in Lincolnshire was slightly later, built in a Jacobethan style and combining elements of Elizabethan and Jacobean architecture and extraordinary

Above: Robert Smirke's Staircase Hall at Eastnor Castle has cast-iron bannisters, plus a wooden chandelier, dragon benches and hall chairs, all dating from the 17th century.

internal features in German Baroque. It was constructed in 1837–45 by Anthony Salvin, later a master of Norman Revival castle-building in the mid-19th century. Today the house, known as Harlaxton College, is the British campus of the University of Evansville, Indiana, USA.

BUCKINGHAM PALACE
AND ST JAMES'S PALACE

Buckingham Palace was originally a town house, built for the Duke of Buckingham in 1702 by William Talman and a gentleman architect by the name of William Winde, on the site of an earlier pre-Civil War residence named Arlington House. George III bought Buckingham House in 1762 as a family residence to which he and Queen Charlotte could escape from court life at St James's Palace. Renaming it the Queen's House, he built a large library. Fourteen of George and Charlotte's 15 children were born in the Queen's House – all except George IV, who was born in St James's Palace.

After his accession in 1820, George IV initially wanted to modernize Buckingham House and to continue using it as a private dwelling. However, in 1826 he decided to convert it into a palace, using designs by John Nash, who had recently completed work on the Royal Pavilion in Brighton.

THE MARBLE ARCH
Nash enlarged the main house, building a new set of rooms on the garden, or west, side and replacing the existing

Below: A view of Buckingham Palace and Marble Arch from St James's Park, c.1835. The arch was moved to Hyde Park in 1851.

Above: This view dates to c.1820, before George IV and John Nash set to work to transform Buckingham House into a palace.

north and south wings, thus creating a U-shaped house enclosing an east-facing courtyard on three sides. He designed the façades of Bath stone in a French Neoclassical style favoured by the King. To use the courtyard, iron railings and a grand Marble Arch, inspired by the Arch of Constantine in Rome, were constructed. The arch was intended partly as a war memorial to Britons killed at the battles of Trafalgar and Waterloo; it was also a tribute to the

King and was intended to support a statue of George IV by Sir Francis Chantrey. However, George died before the work was complete and the statue was finally erected in Trafalgar Square. The arch itself was built in 1827 and formed the eastern entrance to the palace forecourt for almost a quarter of a century, until it was moved in 1851 to its present position, at the north-east corner of Hyde Park.

THE NEW STATEROOMS
Internally, Nash laid out a splendid set of staterooms in Buckingham Palace. From the Grand Hall, the marble Grand Staircase rose to the Picture Gallery in the centre of the block and beyond it to new staterooms on the garden front, with its elegant bow: the Blue Drawing Room, the White Drawing Room and, in the domed bow, the Music Room.

ST JAMES'S PALACE

A stone's throw from Buckingham Palace, St James's Palace is today ranked as the 'senior palace of the sovereign' and is still officially a royal residence. It was largely constructed in red brick by Henry VIII in 1531–6 on the site of the Hospital of St James. Several parts of the original palace survive, including the Chapel Royal and the great Gate House, now at the southern end of St James's Street. For three centuries it was one of the principal royal residences in London, birthplace of Charles II, James II, Mary II, Queen Anne and George IV. After most of Whitehall Palace burned down in 1698, all monarchs spent part of the year at St James's Palace. It was badly damaged by fire in 1809, and George IV undertook a grand refurbishment of its staterooms in the 1820s. William IV was the last monarch to live at St James's; from the reign of Victoria, the ruling monarch has resided in Buckingham Palace when he or she is in London.

Right: The gatehouse of St James's Palace.

Above: Carlton House's Grand Staircase rose majestically beneath a great chandelier.

Below: The lavish surroundings of the Throne Room at Buckingham Palace. Queen Victoria would use it as a second ballroom.

On the east front, facing into the open courtyard, the apartments included the Throne Room and Green Drawing Room. Many of the fittings in these rooms had been salvaged from Carlton House when it was demolished in 1827.

PUBLIC OUTCRY

The designs, amid a clamour for parliamentary reform, were not popular. There was considerable public disquiet over the cost and Nash's perceived extravagance: George IV initially asked for £500,000, but his prime minister agreed to only £150,000 – a sum later increased to £200,000. But when George IV died in 1830, it emerged that the still unfinished work had cost £501,530. The dome on the garden side was ridiculed as 'a wretched inverted egg-cup'.

Following a government investigation, amid concerns that some of the work was not structurally sound, Nash was dismissed, having been judged to be guilty of 'inexcusable irregularity and great negligence'. George's successor, William IV, commissioned the more modest Edward Blore to complete the palace; the well-known east front facing the Mall, which contains the balcony, was added in 1850, then redesigned and refaced in Portland Stone in 1913 by Sir Aston Webb.

THE GRANGE AT NORTHINGTON
AND THE GREEK REVIVAL

The Greek Revival arose following the circulation in the late 18th and early 19th centuries of illustrations of Greek art and architecture and the arrival, in London in 1803, of the 'Elgin Marbles' – fragments of ancient Greek sculpture brought to London by Thomas Bruce, 7th Earl of Elgin, who had been British ambassador to the Ottoman Empire. The British upper classes became convinced of the superiority of ancient Greek sculpture and buildings in comparison with those of other ancient or more modern cultures. The Revival was principally an urban phenomenon – evidenced in town halls,

Below: The Grange's great portico of Doric columns faces east; note also the central block of four square piers and pilasters between the bays on the south side.

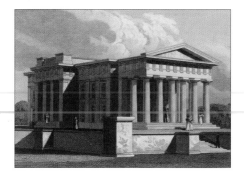

Above: This engraving shows The Grange in 1830, within a quarter-century of its building by William Wilkins in 1804–9.

courts of justice, hospitals, colleges, theatres and other buildings decorated with Greek columns and loosely made to look like Greek temples. The Revival, which swept through Europe, was also particularly popular in the United States, where it became known as the 'National style'.

Above: The original house looks out between columns at The Grange. Pevsner declared the Doric portico to have 'tremendous pathos'.

AN ARCADIAN VISION

A striking early example of Greek Revival style in country-house building was The Grange at Northington, near Winchester in Hampshire. In 1804–9, William Wilkins refashioned an existing 17th-century house in the image of a Greek temple, specifically in the likeness

of the Theseum in Athens. On the east side, overlooking a lake, Wilkins raised a portico consisting of two lines of six great Doric columns. On the north and south sides, each composed of nine bays, he added a central block containing four square piers.

The archaeologist and architect C.R. Cockerell had boundless admiration, writing of The Grange in the early 19th century: 'Nothing can be finer (or) more classical... there is nothing like it on this side of Arcadia.' Today, the house is partly ruined, but the extraordinary portico can still be seen.

JOHN DOBSON

The country house of Meldon Park in Northumberland was built in 1832 by the well-known Newcastle architect John Dobson for Isaac Cookson. Its Ionic entrance porch and clean lines make it a good example of the Greek Revival style.

Dobson was an accomplished town architect, and like Nash in London, the builder of delightful Regency-style townhouses. In Newcastle he built Grainger, Market and Grey Streets and, after completing Meldon Park, constructed the city's acclaimed railway station. At Meldon

Above: Doric columns surround the front door at Arlington Court in Devon. Visitors may try out one of the National Trust's large collection of horse-drawn carriages there.

he produced a studiedly plain exterior that is decorated only by the columns of the entrance porch; all its essential drainpipes and guttering are hidden from view.

MORE REVIVAL HOUSES

Other early examples of the Greek Revival country house include Longford Hall in Shropshire, designed in 1789 by Joseph Bonomi: its portico has four columns and its Great Hall a fine Grecian frieze. In 1803, at Stratton Park in Hampshire, George Dance the Younger built a two-storey portico with vast Doric columns; the house has been demolished but the portico remains as part of a 1960s mansion.

In 1808, Joseph Gandy, the highly talented assistant of Sir John Soane, who so imaginatively illustrated Soane's architectural schemes, built a fine Greek Revival house at Storrs Hall on the shores of Lake Windermere: it has a splendid Doric colonnade on its entrance front. Arlington Court near Barnstaple in Devon was designed with a Doric-columned entranceway and Doric entablature by local architect Thomas Lee for Colonel John Chichester in 1820.

BELSAY HALL, NORTHUMBERLAND

At Belsay Hall, in 1807–15, Sir Charles Monck built an austere square limestone house with a vast Doric portico and a Doric frieze running around the building. Sir Charles had returned in 1806 from a two-year trip to Greece, in which he was greatly impressed by ancient Greek temple architecture. With the help of John Dobson, designer of Meldon Park, Sir Charles set out to create a Greek Revival house for his recently inherited estate. Internally, he laid out the rooms around a central space lit from

above, in the style of a Greek or Roman dwelling. The Belsay Hall estate also contains a 14th-century tower house (called 'the Castle') and the ruins of one wing of a 17th-century house. There are magnificent gardens, partly laid out by Sir Charles himself, including one in the quarry from which his workmen cut out the limestone to build the Hall.

Below: The imposing Doric columns on the main front at Belsay Hall. Note also the Doric frieze running around the building.

RESTORATION AT WINDSOR

UNDER GEORGE IV

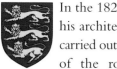

In the 1820s, George IV and his architect Jeffry Wyatville carried out a major restoration of the royal buildings at Windsor, which, combined with earlier work by James Wyatt in 1800–11, created the 'picturesque' Gothic castle we see today. Within the palace, George and Wyatville swept away many of the superb interiors created by Charles II, but they were also responsible for a magnificent series of royal apartments and the creation of the remarkable Waterloo Chamber to house portraits of the military heroes who had defeated Napoleon at the Battle of Waterloo.

GEORGE III AT WINDSOR

In 1778–82, George III and Sir William Chambers rebuilt Queen Anne's Lodge, which stood to the south of the castle's upper ward. Renamed the Queen's Lodge, the building was George and Queen Charlotte's favoured residence at Windsor (it was demolished by George IV in 1823). Within the castle in the 1780s and 90s, he restored St George's Chapel and made improvements to the staterooms, including the addition of

historical paintings of scenes from the life of Edward III by the American artist, Benjamin West.

WYATT'S ADDITIONS

James Wyatt began work for the royal family at Windsor with the rebuilding of Queen Charlotte's House at Frogmore, adjoining Windsor Great Park. George III bought the Frogmore estate for the

Above: The Green Drawing Room is one of the splendid set of new rooms that was created by Wyatville in the castle's east front.

Queen in 1790 and Wyatt impressed both with his work there in the 1790s. In 1800–11, he was commissioned to rebuild the state apartments in the castle's upper ward in the Gothic style. He put in pointed Gothic windows to replace those inserted by Hugh May in the 17th century, constructed a cloister in Horn Court and raised a splendid entrance from the quadrangle. He also installed a Grand Staircase to replace the former 'King's Stair' and created a suite of private rooms on the ground floor of the north block. In these rooms, George III was confined in his final illness.

WINDSOR TRANSFORMED

The Prince Regent used John Nash to rebuild the Lower Lodge, situated about 3 miles (4.5km) south-east of the castle in the Great Park, as the Royal Lodge.

Left: The State Dining Room. Both this and the Green Drawing Room were restored after the damage caused by fire in 1992.

The Prince lived there while at Windsor, but following his father's death in 1820 he moved into the castle, and began a new round of rebuilding. Jeffry Wyatt, nephew of James Wyatt, won a competition in 1823, whose details had been drafted by Sir Charles Long, to take on the work. (Although now referred to as Jeffry Wyatville, the architect was known by his original name until 1824, when he changed his name to Wyatville in line with the taste for the Gothic; he was knighted in 1828.)

In the upper ward, Wyatville added a battlemented upper storey to the south-east and north sides of the quadrangle. He moved the private apartments from the north to the south and east sections. The north-side rooms were set aside for state occasions.

In the east front, he created a superb set of royal rooms, including the Dining Room and the White and Crimson Drawing Rooms, which are as grand as any of the interiors lost for posterity when Carlton House in London was demolished. Indeed, these rooms at Windsor, like the apartments in Buckingham Palace, contain several fittings and pieces of furniture salvaged

LONGLEAT HOUSE

Jeffry Wyatville is also remembered for his work at Longleat House – the 16th-century 'prodigy house' in Wiltshire built by the Elizabethan courtier Sir John Thynne. In 1806–14, Wyatville reconstructed the north front, built a magnificent Grand Staircase to connect the two inner courtyards and redecorated several rooms. Among other houses on which he worked were Chatsworth House, where he built an extension to the north wing in 1820–41, and Fort Belvedere in Windsor Great Park, famously the home of Edward, Prince of Wales, briefly Edward VIII and later Duke of Windsor, where he added extensions in 1827–30.

from Carlton House. Along the inner and south front of the quadrangle, he created the splendid Grand Corridor, more than 500ft (150m) in length. He raised the height of the Round Tower by around 30ft (9m), and remodelled the outer walls of the upper ward's south wing, creating a distinctive symmetrical façade for the castle.

WATERLOO CHAMBER

Wyatville created the Waterloo Chamber by roofing in the former Horn Court. Here, he placed some Grinling Gibbons' carving removed from the Charles II-era Royal Chapel, and hung specially commissioned portraits by Sir Thomas Lawrence of royal and military figures associated with Wellington's triumph at Waterloo – including Georges III and IV, the Duke of Wellington and Field Marshall von Blücher.

LONGER WALK

As part of Wyatville's rebuilding, the Long Walk created by King Charles II to link the castle to Windsor Great Park was lengthened in 1823 to run right up to a new entranceway,

Above: Windsor Castle from the Great Park. The 19th-century work at Windsor created a skyline in the Picturesque Gothic.

the George IV Gateway. This entailed knocking down King George III's Queen's Lodge. (See also page 68.)

Below: This 19th-century aquatint shows the castle's sweeping Grand Staircase shortly after its completion.

CHAPTER THREE

VICTORIAN STYLE

*c.*1830–1901

On 27 August 1839, the 13th Earl of Eglington held a medieval tournament complete with jousting in the lists at Eglington Castle in Ayrshire. A great crowd of spectators in medieval costume saw Lady Eglington – styled the 'Queen of Beauty' – receive the chivalrous offerings of mounted knights. Unfortunately, after these preliminaries, Scottish rain sweeping in from the west was the winner, for the competition was washed away by a great noon downpour that obscured visibility and reduced the lists to a mud bath. But the tournament at Eglington was a remarkable reflection of an aristocratic interest in the cult of chivalry and medieval life that resulted in the rebuilding of many country homes in the style of castles.

At Cardiff Castle and Castell Coch in Wales, John Crichton Stuart, the 3rd Marquess of Bute, and his architect William Burges produced exquisite romantic recreations of the medieval castle. Likewise, at Arundel in Sussex and at Alnwick in Northumberland, the dukes of Norfolk and Northumberland and their architects 'improved' the ruins of their ancient strongholds and castles to create picturesque turreted skylines and sumptuous interiors. Certainly not least among these ambitious essays in the revival castle was the rebuilding by Queen Victoria's husband, Prince Albert, at Balmoral, in which he turned a modest country house on the River Dee in Scotland into a turreted fairy-tale fortress in the Scottish Baronial style.

Left: Arundel Castle ranks below only Windsor and Alnwick as a supreme example of the Romantic recreation of the Middle Ages by Georgian and Victorian architects.

BUCKINGHAM PALACE
THE OFFICIAL LONDON RESIDENCE OF QUEEN VICTORIA

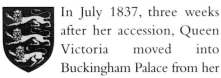

In July 1837, three weeks after her accession, Queen Victoria moved into Buckingham Palace from her childhood home at Kensington. She made the palace the monarch's official London residence. Shortly after moving in, she put in train a number of improvements to make her quarters more private; as part of these works Nash's unpopular dome (previously derided as 'a wretched inverted egg-cup') was removed (see pages 52–3).

A NEW EAST WING

On Victoria's marriage in 1840 to Prince Albert of Saxe-Coburg-Gotha, it became clear that the lack of nursery accommodation in the palace would be a problem; in addition, the state apartments of George IV were found to be too small to hold a court ball. In 1847–50, the famous London builder, Thomas Cubitt, constructed a new wing along the east side of the palace courtyard, facing the Mall. It was designed by Edward Blore, with nurseries on the top floor and apartments for prominent visitors on the first floor. The building work was

partly funded by the sale of Brighton Pavilion, and the interiors of the new wing also made use of furnishings and fittings from the Pavilion, notably in the Chinese decorations of the Luncheon Room and the East Room. To make room for the new wing, the Marble Arch was moved to its present position

Above: The palace Ballroom as it looked on completion in c. 1855. It has since been redecorated in white with gold details.

at the north-east corner of Hyde Park, formerly the site of the Tyburn gallows. Blore used a soft French stone that proved vulnerable to the weather and London atmosphere, and the east wing of the palace was refaced with Portland stone just before World War I by Sir Aston Webb (see page 76).

A LAVISH BALLROOM

The required Ballroom was added, together with a State Supper Room and new galleries, on the west front of the palace. This work was designed by James Pennethorne, a pupil of the disgraced John Nash, and built in 1852–5 by Cubitt. The impressive Ballroom measured 123 x 60ft (37 x 18m). The interior was lavishly decorated, under the guidance of Prince Albert, as advised by his artistic designer, Professor Ludwig Grüner, with murals by Niccola Consoni and sculptures by William Theed.

THE ROYAL MEWS

The Royal Mews in Buckingham Palace Road, which house the Queen's carriages, horses and motor vehicles, were built in 1824–5 by John Nash, with two Doric arches and two sets of stables as well as grand coach-houses.

The Mews had been established in this location in 1760 by George III: Sir William Chambers built an indoor riding school there in 1763–6. In 1855, Victoria added a school on the site for the children of Royal Mews staff, and in 1859 constructed further accommodation there. Visitors to the Mews can see the gold state coach built for George III to designs by Sir William Chambers in 1762 and used for all coronations since.

Left: The gold state coach of George III, used for coronations and state occasions.

BALMORAL
AND THE SCOTTISH BARONIAL STYLE

Queen Victoria and Prince Albert bought the estate and modest manor house of Balmoral on the River Dee in the Grampian region of Scotland in 1852. Albert and architect William Smith at once demolished the existing house and in 1853–5 built a turreted castle in the Scottish Baronial style.

The Queen and her husband had fallen in love with Scotland during holidays at Taymouth and Blair Atholl in the early 1840s. They leased Balmoral and stayed there for the first time in the autumn of 1848. Their initial visit was a great success, although the original house – called 'a pretty little castle in the old Scotch style' by Victoria – was too small for their needs: members of the royal household had to stay in nearby

Below: Balmoral has been a favoured royal retreat since Prince Albert designed it and Victoria described it as 'this dear paradise'.

cottages and wait each morning for their breakfast to be delivered by wheelbarrow from the main house.

A COUNTRY HOUSE

Albert set out to design a holiday retreat rather than a grand royal residence, in his words a building 'not like a palace but like a country gentleman's house'. In contrast to Osborne House, Balmoral has no Audience Chamber or Council Room in which the Queen may receive ministers and other officials; there are only general-purpose rooms for significant visitors on the south side of the main block's ground floor. Otherwise, the main block contains the Dining Room, Drawing Room, Billiard Room and Library, with private rooms for the Queen and Prince on the floor above. Throughout, as at Osborne House, the most modern conveniences were provided, with hot-air heating, four bathrooms for the royal family and 14

BELFAST CASTLE

Above: The 19th-century Scots Baronial house stands on the site of a Norman fortification and a 17th-century castle.

Prince Albert's work at Balmoral set a fashion for the Scottish Baronial architectural style. In the light of this and as a way of underlining Ulster's connection to Scotland, the architect W.H. Lynn used the same romantic blend of gables and turrets for Belfast Castle, built in a beautiful position overlooking the city, for the 3rd Marquess of Donegall and his wealthy son-in-law, Lord Ashley, in 1867–70.

water-closets – at the time, a record for a British country house. There was also a servants' wing, stables and offices.

Victoria and Albert moved into the main house in September 1855, and returned each autumn until Albert's death in 1861. After that dark event, Victoria often visited twice a year: in June and from August to November. The place had special significance because of its association with her husband: it was, she wrote, 'Albert's own creation, own work, own building, own laying out', and she added 'my dearest Albert's … great taste and the impress of his dear hand have been stamped everywhere'.

OSBORNE HOUSE
VICTORIA'S FAVOURITE HOUSE

Queen Victoria's favourite royal residence was the palatial seaside villa of Osborne House on the Isle of Wight. At Osborne – designed and built by her beloved husband, Prince Albert, in collaboration with Thomas Cubitt – she spent many of her happiest hours of family life and here, at the end of a long and highly productive reign, she died on 22 January 1901 surrounded by her children and grandchildren.

Victoria wanted a seaside retreat but intensely disliked the Royal Pavilion in Brighton, with its associations with the extravagant and colourful private life of George IV and which had been engulfed by the growth of the resort and therefore lacked privacy. She decided to sell the Pavilion and to buy a house and estate on the Isle of Wight, which she knew from happy childhood visits to Norris Castle in 1831 and 1833.

With the help of her then prime minister, Sir Robert Peel, Victoria and Albert found Osborne House, overlooking the Solent on the north

side of the Isle of Wight, and, after a successful stay in 1843, the royal couple purchased the 1,000 acre (405 ha)-estate – which came with its own private beach as well as a substantial Georgian house – from Lady Isabella Blanchford in 1845. Victoria wrote of her pleasure at having 'a place of one's own, quiet and retired'.

Above: Palazzo style. The view from the Lower Terrace, with the Andromeda Fountain, back up to the Clock Tower.

AN ITALIANATE VILLA

The Queen and Prince Albert demolished the existing house, and, with Cubitt, who had made his reputation developing Highbury and Belgravia in London, Albert built a splendid Italianate villa in 1845–51. Osborne's design, with two *campanile* towers, was a tribute to the Italian Renaissance *palazzo* (palace) and influenced by a pair of villas built by Sir Charles Barry: Mount Felix at Walton-on-Thames, Surrey (1836), and Trentham Hall in north Staffordshire (1842). Its façades mixed Roman, Florentine and Palladian elements to charming effect. When he visited Osborne, the twice prime minister, Benjamin Disraeli, was enraptured, describing it as 'a Sicilian Palazzo with garden terraces, statues and vases shining in the sun, than which nothing can be conceived more captivating'.

The house was laid out, with the privacy of the royal family in mind, in two main parts: a rectangular Family Pavilion for the Queen, Albert and children

BRODSWORTH HALL

The Italianate *palazzo* style used by Prince Albert at Osborne House was widely influential. A particularly fine example is Brodsworth Hall in South Yorkshire, designed for Charles Thellusson by an unknown Italian architect, Chevalier Casentini, in 1861–3. Casentini replaced the original 18th-century hall with an elegant but very substantial villa containing more than 30 rooms.

The house has been maintained carefully since it was taken over from its last owner, a Thellusson descendant, by English Heritage in 1990 and is one of the least altered of all Victorian country houses. The estate has fine

Above: Casentini did not visit Yorkshire. His design for Brodsworth was implemented by English architect, Philip Wilkinson.

gardens with an Italian-style fountain and statue walks, summerhouse, woodland, ornamental flowerbeds and a quarry area – all restored since 1990 to their 1860s' condition and plan.

Above: At Osborne, where she had often retreated following the loss of Albert, Victoria lay in state after her own death.

linked by the grand Marble Corridor to a substantial and asymetrical east wing, intended for visitors and members of the royal household.

The Family Pavilion was built in 1845 and splendidly fitted out in 1846, and the royal family moved in during September of that year. On their first night of residence, Prince Albert led prayers seeking God's blessing on the house and recited sections of a Lutheran hymn.

The German art professor, Ludwig Grüner, acting as Prince Albert's artistic designer from 1845, was in charge of decorating the interior of the Family Pavilion. Its most splendid section was without doubt the Marble Corridor, which featured floor tiles designed by Prince Albert and polychrome stencilling on the walls in blue, umber, black and red. Along the walls were displayed Albert's collection of contemporary sculptures by artists including R.J. Wyatt and John Gibson.

Prince Albert believed that English country houses were generally too gloomy, so he designed the three main rooms on the ground floor of the Family Pavilion with large plate-glass windows. These rooms are the Dining Room, the Drawing Room and the

Right: Italian towers and terraces look down on formal gardens at Osborne House and have beautiful views of the Solent.

Billiard Room, the last two divided only by Corinthian columns in yellow marble, together essentially forming one sizeable L-shaped room. The Drawing Room contains a bow window giving fine views over the terraced gardens to the Solent.

On the first floor was a private suite designed for the Queen and Prince Albert, consisting of two bathrooms, two dressing rooms, a bedroom and a sitting room. Above that, on the second floor, were the nursery rooms. Albert and Cubitt also co-operated in the design of formal terraced gardens at Osborne in 1847. The grounds included a Swiss Cottage – a miniature dwelling designed as a playhouse for the royal children.

INDIAN HALL

Towards the end of Queen Victoria's reign, after she had become Empress of India in 1877 and was taking a significant interest in Indian affairs, a new wing was added at Osborne House in 1890–1. Its ground floor consisted of a large Reception Hall decorated in Indian style by imported craftsmen and designed by Bhai Ram Singh, an expert on Indian architecture, with advice from Rudyard Kipling's father, John Lockwood Kipling, who was director of Lahore Central Museum. Called the Durbar Hall, the new building featured elaborate Moghul-style plasterwork. Above the Reception Hall, on the second floor of the wing, were apartments for Victoria's youngest daughter, Princess Beatrice, and her family.

A MODERN HOUSE

Throughout Osborne House, Cubitt used the most up-to-date materials, providing the very latest plumbing and central-heating systems. Also in 1890, electric lights were fitted throughout Osborne House.

Victoria's son and successor Edward VII disliked Osborne House and donated it to the nation. Her apartments have been open to the public since 1954.

ALNWICK, EASTNOR AND ARUNDEL
GREAT VICTORIAN CASTLE REVIVALS

In the 1850s, the architect Anthony Salvin and Algernon Percy, 4th Duke of Northumberland, substantially rebuilt the great Percy stronghold of Alnwick Castle in Northumberland, adding both the imposing Prudhoe Tower and the North Terrace. Salvin's very impressive rebuilding, which swept away much of the Georgian Gothic remodelling carried out at Alnwick in the 18th century by Robert Adam, was one of the greatest of a swathe of Victorian castle revivals undertaken in the mid-19th century.

ALNWICK'S HISTORY
The first castle on the site was built in 1096 by Yves de Vescy, Baron of Alnwick. Strongly fortified in the next century, it twice repelled sieges by William I 'the Lion' of Scots; on the second occasion, in 1174, 'the Lion' was

Below: In the 1860s, Anthony Salvin converted the courtyard at Muncaster Castle into the barrel-vaulted Drawing Room.

taken prisoner in fog outside the castle and thrown into jail. The first Percy ancestor at Alnwick, Henry, 1st Lord Percy, bought the castle in 1309 and began its restoration.

Of this work, one semicircular tower survives today (of the seven that initially comprised the keep), as does much of the curtain wall, several other towers and the gateway that stands between the two baileys. Later Percys were to suffer for their Roman Catholic faith: Thomas Percy, 7th Earl of Northumberland, lost his head for his part in the 'Rising of the North' against Queen Elizabeth I.

In the 17th century, the castle fell into decay, but it was rebuilt and modernized by Sir Hugh Smithson and Percy heiress, Lady Betty Seymour, later the 1st Duke and Duchess of Northumberland, in the mid-18th century. At the same time they commissioned Robert Adam to redecorate Syon House in Middlesex. At Alnwick, they employed Adam alongside James Paine to work in the

Above: For all the rebuilding and restoration work, Alnwick Castle retains its original plan – of a motte and two baileys.

Georgian Gothic Revival style, remnants of which include the life-size stone figures on the battlements.

THE 4TH DUKE'S ADDITIONS
In 1847, and at the age of 55, Algernon Percy succeeded his brother Hugh as 4th Duke of Northumberland towards the end of a very busy and fruitful life in which he had served in the navy during the Napoleonic Wars and had, subsequently, been one of the first Englishmen to excavate the tombs of ancient Egypt. He displayed several of his archaeological finds in the Castle Museum at Alnwick, established in the Postern Tower and opened to the public as early as 1826.

In their rebuilding of Alnwick, Salvin and the 4th Duke constructed a new chapel, the Guest Hall, the Falconer's Tower and a riding school with stables, in addition to the great Prudhoe Tower. The Duke combined the castle's rugged Gothic Revival exterior with the most luxurious Italian Renaissance-style interiors, including widely admired coffered ceilings and superb scarlet damask and gold hangings in the Drawing Room. Within the Prudhoe Tower, he installed a fine Library and, in the place of the medieval Great Hall, created a Dining Hall with a wonderful carved, unpainted pine and cedar ceiling.

ANTHONY SALVIN

Salvin, architect of the extraordinary 'Jacobethan-Baroque' Harlaxton Manor in Lincolnshire in 1837–45, ably extended and rebuilt a large number of castles for Victorian patrons. These included Muncaster Castle, overlooking the River Esk near Ravenglass in Cumbria, where he worked for Gamel Augustus Pennington, 4th Lord Muncaster, from 1862 onward. Salvin converted the courtyard into the fine Drawing Room with barrel ceiling, built a north-west tower to match the 14th-century pele tower at the south-west of the site and added battlements and transomed and mullioned windows.

Another of Salvin's notable commissions was Peckforton Castle in Tarporley, west Cheshire. Peckforton was a new country house built in the style of a medieval castle for MP John Tollemache (subsequently Lord Tollemache) in 1844–51. Its centrepiece was the Great Hall, with stone vaulted ceiling, minstrels' gallery and intricately carved screen; the main reception rooms gave on to a splendid pentagonal stairwell.

EASTNOR CASTLE

In Herefordshire, John Somers Cocks, 1st Earl Somers, and the architect Robert Smirke built the vast Eastnor Castle in a Norman Revival style in 1810–20. At this time timber was in short supply because it was being used to build ships for the Royal Navy to

Below: Social unrest persuaded John Tollemache that Peckforton Castle should be fit to withstand a siege.

repel an expected Napoleonic invasion, so Smirke used cast iron for roof trusses and in place of large beams. The main building material was a handsome sandstone, brought from quarries in the Forest of Dean by canal and then mule. Smirke created a simple, medieval-style interior. The 1st Earl's descendants

Above: The great Gothic Revivalist A. W. Pugin created this magnificent 'medieval' Drawing Room at Eastnor Castle in 1849.

added to this, commissioning a superb Gothic drawing room in 1849 and lavish work in the Long Library and State Bedroom in the 1860-70s.

ARUNDEL CASTLE

Arundel Castle in West Sussex stands on a Norman motte (of 1068), and contains a medieval gatehouse and barbican, but it is primarily a Victorian recreation of the Middle Ages. This magnificent achievement is in small part the work of Charles Howard, the 11th Duke of Norfolk, and architect Francis Hiorne in 1791-1815, and in large part the creation of Henry Fitzalan-Howard, the 15th Duke, and architect CA Buckler in 1870-1900. The superb Gothic library, with its vaulted roof of mahogany, was built by Jonathan Ritson in 1802. Buckler's chapel is celebrated as one of the best Victorian Gothic interiors. The 15th Duke also equipped the castle with 'mod cons' – Arundel was one of the pioneers of fitting electricity and central heating in English country houses.

Above: Purists may dismiss many Victorian 'improvements' of England's medieval legacy, but it is impossible not to admire the Gothic chapel at Arundel.

CARDIFF CASTLE AND CASTELL COCH
WILLIAM BURGES AND CONJECTURAL RESTORATION

John Crichton Stuart, 3rd Marquess of Bute, was said to be the richest man in the world in the 1860s. He had inherited a vast fortune, derived partly from the export of Welsh coal from Cardiff, as an infant in 1848. In 1866, aged only 19, he commissioned architect William Burges to rebuild Cardiff Castle in an opulent Victorian Gothic style.

ROMAN AND NORMAN REMAINS
The castle stands in the centre of Cardiff, on the site of a Roman fort and a Norman stronghold. Remains from both these periods are incorporated into the building: approaching the main entrance, for example, Roman stonework is visible at the base of Norman walls, while within the enclosure the Norman shell keep still stands proudly on its motte. For centuries, the castle was an important fortress, passing from one powerful lord to another: the de Clare family in the 12–13th centuries; Hugh le Despenser in the reign of Edward II; Richard Neville, Earl of Warwick ('the Kingmaker'), and Richard, Duke of Gloucester (later Richard III), in the 15th century; and the Herbert

Below: The Gothic towers and crenellations of Bute and Burges combine with Roman and Norman stonework at Cardiff Castle.

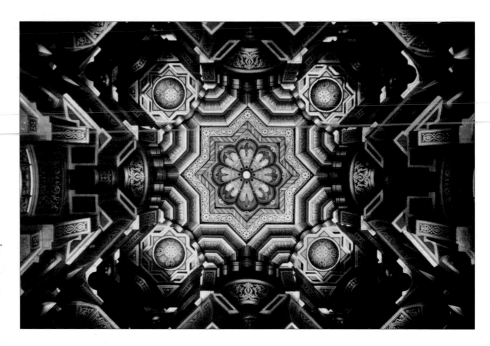

lords in the 16th century. It was finally passed by marriage into the hands of the Bute family in 1766.

THEMED ROOMS
Bute and Burges raised Gothic towers and created elaborate interiors with stained glass, murals, wood and stone carving and marble fireplaces. A number of the rooms were elaborately themed: the Winter Smoking Room, for example, has the theme of passing time, being decorated with images of the seasons and days of the week.

THREE GREAT TOWERS
The work on Cardiff Castle was complemented by Bute and Burges' equally lavish restoration of the Marquess's country retreat near Cardiff – the 13th-century castle of Castell Coch. Beginning in 1875, Burges built almost from scratch, for the original fortress had been reduced to ruins in the 15th century. He raised three great towers with conical roofs: the Keep Tower, next to the gatehouse, was linked to the Kitchen Tower by the Banqueting Hall; the curtain wall then followed an irregular circle around to the Well Tower.

Above: Kaleidoscope of colours – a detail of the fantastically elaborate decoration in the Arabian Room, Cardiff Castle.

The castle was compact, its three towers grouped around a courtyard only 55ft (17m) across. It stood within a dry moat and, with great attention to medieval detail, was fitted with a portcullis and a drawbridge, as well as murder-holes for pouring boiling water or oil on to intruders.

Below: Eastern promise. Beautiful blue-black floor tiles combine with delicate carving in this lavish interior at Cardiff Castle.

Left: The reddish sandstone used at Castell Coch, near Cardiff, gives the building its popular name of the 'Red Castle'.

of animals and birds and, above the splendid tiled fireplace, exquisitely carved figures of the Three Fates from ancient Greek mythology. A raised balcony runs around the second-storey level and a beautiful azure and gold vaulted ceiling painted with stars and birds rises above.

On the third and fourth floors of the tower, beneath a double dome ceiling, is the Lady's Bedroom, decorated with gilt and mirrors and containing a

remarkable 'Moorish' bed fitted with eight crystal balls and derived from the interiors of the Alhambra in Granada, Spain. Other rooms include the more austere Banqueting Hall, the Lord's Bedroom, the Servants' Hall and kitchen. All the work at Castell Coch was meticulously researched by Burges in the British Museum for historical accuracy, and he wrote extensive justifications of this 'conjectural restoration'.

Below: The two-storey Drawing Room at Castell Coch. Note the Three Fates above the fireplace, the painted panels and the balcony beneath the domed azure ceiling.

LAVISH DECORATION

As at Cardiff Castle, the interiors were lavishly finished; many were, in fact, not decorated under the architect's supervision, for he died in 1881, but were overseen by William Frame working from Burges' detailed plans for the decor. The Keep Tower contains a two-storey Drawing Room, decorated with scenes from Aesop's Fables: delicate painted panels depicting plants, mouldings

CARLTON TOWERS

Carlton Towers at Goole in North Yorkshire was twice 'Gothicized' in the Victorian era, creating one of the most celebrated of Victorian Gothic country houses. The original Jacobean house of 1614 was initially remodelled in 1840 by Miles, the 8th Lord Beaumont, before it was reworked more substantially, in 1873–6, by E. W. Pugin (son of Augustus Welby Pugin) for Henry, 9th Lord Beaumont. Then, after Lord Beaumont quarrelled with his architect, he commissioned John Francis Bentley, the Roman Catholic architect of Westminster Cathedral, to decorate the interior. The result was a superb suite of staterooms that incorporated the Armoury, Venetian Drawing Room, Card Room and Picture Gallery.

WINDSOR CASTLE AND FROGMORE
VICTORIA AND ALBERT

Queen Victoria and Prince Albert are particularly associated with Osborne House and Balmoral, but in fact they spent the majority of each year at Windsor, where Albert was a Ranger of the Great Park and carried out a number of improvements on the estate. He worked in the Home Park, encompassing the Frogmore estate and Shaw Farm to the north of the castle, as well as in the Great Park. In particular, he rebuilt the Home Farm in 1852 in a Tudor Revival style and in 1858 reconstructed George III's dairy building with an admired interior featuring Minton tiles and sculpture by John Thomas (see also page 56).

ALBERT MEMORIALS

However, the most significant building work at Windsor Castle during Victoria's reign was carried out in memory of Albert, who died of typhoid fever there on 14 December 1861. Victoria insisted that Albert's rooms were kept exactly as they had been on the day of his death, and rebuilt the chapel that stood above

Below: An aerial view of Windsor Castle shows the upper ward to the right and the lower ward to the left of the Round Tower.

PRIVATE BURIAL

Victoria broke with royal tradition in being buried in a mausoleum on private ground rather than in a cathedral or major church. The idea of a mausoleum had come from her Uncle Leopold, who built one at Claremont for his wife, Princess Charlotte – which in turn inspired Prince Albert to raise one at Coburgh for his father and Victoria to construct one for her mother, the Duchess of Kent, also at Frogmore. After Victoria's death, the former Edward VIII was buried at Frogmore following his death in 1972 and his wife, Wallis, the woman for whom he gave up the throne, was buried alongside him in 1986.

Above: Windsor's Albert Memorial. On her death in 1901, Victoria joined her late husband in the Frogmore Mausoleum.

the Tomb House (behind St George's Chapel) as the magnificent Albert Memorial Chapel. This work was carried out in 1863–73, principally by George Gilbert Scott, who installed fine stained-glass windows and marble reliefs by Jules Destréez on the walls.

At Frogmore, Victoria built a mausoleum for her husband and herself. Designed by Ludwig Grüner and built by A.J. Humbert in 1862–71, the mausoleum has a granite and Portland stone exterior with gunmetal doors; the interior features frescoes by Italian and German painters in the style of Italian Renaissance master Raphael, whom Albert had considered the finest of all artists. The sarcophagus is of marble, granite and bronze and bears effigies of Albert and Victoria, both carved in the 1860s, although Victoria's was, of course, not put in place until her death in 1901.

CHATSWORTH
AND JOSEPH PAXTON

William, 6th Duke of Devonshire, began a 19-year programme of alterations at Chatsworth House, Derbyshire, in 1818. Sir Jeffry Wyatville began by remaking the Long Gallery as a Library, then added a new north wing to the house (in 1820–7), containing the Theatre, Sculpture Gallery, Dining Room and offices. He redecorated the staterooms in 1832–42 and proceeded to work on the Duke's private apartments in the west front. In October 1832, the first stage of Wyatville's redecoration was inspected by the future Queen Victoria, who, aged 13, was entertained to dinner in the new, lavish gold and white Dining Room with her mother, the Duchess of Kent.

GARDENS TRANSFORMED

The Duke appointed the 23-year-old Joseph Paxton – future designer of the Crystal Palace – as Head Gardener at Chatsworth House in 1826. He had met Paxton in Chiswick, where the Horticultural Society gardens the young man managed abutted the grounds of Chiswick House, which the Duke had inherited, along with the other Devonshire estates, in 1811. Paxton

Below: Chatsworth's Long Gallery, remade by Wyatville as a Long Library, offers exercise for both the body and the mind.

Above: The Emperor Fountain, installed by Paxton in 1844, can send its waters twice as high as the house behind.

transformed the gardens at Chatsworth, creating a vast rock garden, planting rare species from around the world and experimenting with glasshouses and heating apparatus to help them flourish in Derbyshire. His extraordinary Great Conservatory, built in 1840 (and demolished in 1920), was the forerunner of the Crystal Palace. Paxton also designed and installed the Emperor Fountain, capable of launching a water jet to a height of 298ft (90m), and so called because its installation was intended to

mark a visit to Chatsworth by Tsar Nicolas I of Russia, though in the event the visit did not take place.

The 6th Duke spent lavishly at Chatsworth and by his death in 1858 owed a massive £1,000,000. Yet debt did not detract from the great pleasure he received from the house and gardens: 'What happiness I have in Chatsworth, adorable Chatsworth, happiness beyond words.' He entertained continuously on a grand scale: notable visitors included Queen Victoria and Prince Albert.

Below: In addition to building glasshouses, Paxton also dug a coal tunnel in the gardens, which has recently been excavated.

KNEBWORTH HOUSE
AND HUGHENDEN MANOR

Edward Bulwer Lytton, author of best-selling historical novels and former Member of Parliament, inherited Knebworth House on the death of his mother, Elizabeth, in 1843. The original house was a quadrangular brick manor built by a distant ancestor, Sir Robert Lytton, in 1492; this had been reduced to a single wing rebuilt in the Regency Gothic style and covered in stucco by Mrs Bulwer Lytton in 1811–16. Employing the architect H.E. Kendall Junior and the decorator John G. Crace, Edward added pinnacles, towers, gargoyles and heraldic decorations. In the State Presence Room (now known as the State Drawing Room), Crace designed a Victorian Gothic chimney-piece and over-mantel, installed Tudor rose panelling and fine stained glass with a portrait of Henry VII, and fitted 44 coats of arms into the ceiling. This room survives and is, as Crace designed it to be, 'very Gothic'. The Tudor connection arose because some ancestral

Below: The main façade of Knebworth House, showing the towers and crenellation added by Edward Bulwer Lytton.

research revealed that one of Bulwer Lytton's ancestors on his mother's side was an aunt of Henry VII.

HUGHENDEN MANOR
The country house of Hughenden Manor, in Buckinghamshire, was the home from 1848 to his death in 1881 of Benjamin Disraeli, a favourite of Queen Victoria and twice Conservative prime minister (1868 and 1874–80). Queen Victoria visited Hughenden Manor in 1877 – the year after Disraeli

Above: Edward Bulwer Lytton's study at Knebworth House. He was a highly popular and influential writer in his day.

Left: Disraeli followed the fashion for rebuilding an old house in Gothic style.

had secured her the title she longed for, that of 'Empress of India' – and again in 1881, following his death, to lay a wreath on the vault containing his body in the local church. She later erected a memorial to Disraeli in the church.

Hughenden's main interest lies in its association with 'Dizzy'. The house, bought by the rising politician in 1848 for £35,000, was originally a modest farmhouse but was rebuilt in the Gothic style by John Norris in the 1840s. In 1862, the architect Edward Buckton Lamb made a number of alterations, in particular adding pinnacles to relieve the stark outline of the main façade. The gardens were laid out by Disraeli's beloved wife, Mary Anne, now carefully restored to their Victorian prime by the National Trust.

Within, the house is kept as a museum of Disraeli's life and times. It contains a wealth of mementoes of his career as statesman, including a fan signed by all the representatives at the Berlin Congress of 1878, and in the hall – which he called his 'Gallery of Friendship' – hang portraits of several leading political figures of the 19th century. His study remains substantially as he left it.

SANDRINGHAM
AND YORK COTTAGE

Albert Edward, Prince of Wales and the future Edward VII, bought the house and estate at Sandringham, in Norfolk, in 1862 for £220,000. The next spring he settled there with his new wife, Princess Alexandra of Denmark.

The idea of a country home for Albert Edward had begun with his father, Prince Albert, who thought that time spent in outdoor pursuits, such as shooting, would be a healthy change for the Prince of Wales, and that country life would help him keep away from the temptations of city delights, such as courtesans and gambling. However, following Prince Albert's death in December 1861, it was left to his son to complete the search for a house. He chose Sandringham after a single viewing on 3 February 1862.

HUMBERT'S NEW HOUSE

After making do with minor amendments for a few years, the Prince of Wales decided in 1870 to knock down the existing house and start from scratch. He used one of his late father's favoured architects, A.J. Humbert, who, employing red brick with stone dressings, built a large and entirely uninspiring house in a Jacobean Revival style with gables, mullion windows and turrets.

Below: Jacobean style at Sandringham. Houses such as Blickling Hall were the model for A.J. Humbert's design here.

Above: Sandringham sits in 60 acres of gardens. After a bomb from a German zeppelin made a crater in 1915, King George VI had it turned into a duck pond.

YORK COTTAGE

A second architect, R.W. Edis, made additions, including a bowling alley and the Ballroom in 1883 and in the next decade added a new top storey to the house following a fire that broke out during the Prince of Wales's 50th birthday party in 1891. Edis also built a villa, later called York Cottage, in the grounds.

Edward VII's second son, Prince George, Duke of York and the future King George V, moved into York Cottage in 1893 following his marriage to Princess Mary of Teck. It was George's favourite house, reputedly because its modest rooms reminded him of cabins aboard ship and recalled the enjoyable years he had spent in the Royal Navy. Indeed, after his accession he always stayed in York Cottage when visiting, and left the big house to his widowed mother until she died in 1925. George V also died at Sandringham in January 1936.

Born at York Cottage, George VI felt particularly at home on the estate. He wrote to his mother, Queen Mary,

'I have always been so happy here, and I love the place'. He too died at Sandringham House, on 6 February 1952. Elizabeth II made many visits to Sandringham during her childhood and continues to enjoy her Norfolk estate as a welcome country retreat.

CHRISTMAS AT SANDRINGHAM

By the 1930s, Sandringham had become established as the royals' Christmas and New Year retreat. George V made his first Christmas broadcast live by radio on Christmas Day 1932, while, 25 years later, Elizabeth II delivered the first televised Christmas message from the Library.

Below: In November 1902, a royal shooting party gathered at Sandringham during the visit of Germany's Kaiser Wilhelm II.

CHAPTER FOUR

THE COUNTRY HOUSE REVIVAL

1901–TODAY

On his death in 1940, Philip Henry Kerr, 11th Marquess of Lothian, bequeathed his handsome Jacobean mansion of Blickling Hall, Norfolk, to the National Trust. It was the first house to be passed to the Trust under the Country House Scheme of 1937, which Lothian had helped establish, and which enabled owners to leave their property to the Trust in lieu of death duties.

In the 20th century, although country houses continued to be built and lavishly remodelled, and although King Edward VII and his descendants continued to rework Buckingham Palace and other royal residences, many landed families struggled to maintain their houses and estates. Taxes mounted, depression in agriculture ran almost continuously from 1875 to the outbreak of World War II and rental income from land declined. As a result, art collections were broken up and rare library collections sold off to pay for repairs and meet demands for taxes and death duties. Eventually, in the interwar years, some people began to focus on ways to preserve the more historic houses and their collections. By the end of the 20th century, the National Trust carefully maintained and preserved around 350 stately homes, buildings and gardens.

Among new country houses built in these years, the fashion was predominantly neo-Georgian. Buildings such as Castle Drogo and Eaton Hall proved the exception, while neo-Palladian designs, such as Arundel Park, were generally considered more appropriate for a house expected to take its place at the heart of a country estate.

Left: Julius Charles Drewe, immensely wealthy founder of a chain of grocery shops, sought immortality in stone with Castle Drogo, Devon, built by Edwin Lutyens in 1912–30.

ELVEDEN HALL, POLESDEN LACEY
AND THE ROTHSCHILD MANSIONS

In the first years of the 20th century, the great Irish philanthropist and businessman, the 1st Earl of Iveagh, immensely wealthy head of the Guinness brewing dynasty of Dublin, lavishly rebuilt his recently acquired country house, Elveden Hall in Suffolk. It contained, in the Indian Hall (1900–3), perhaps the grandest of several great marble halls created in the Edwardian era. It was sufficiently magnificent for Edward VII to agree to spend every other New Year week there – in alternation with Chatsworth.

Lord Iveagh bought Elveden Hall in 1894 following the death of its previous owner, the former Indian maharajah, Prince Duleep Singh. Removed by the British from his throne following the annexation of the Punjab in 1849, the Prince had been granted a substantial government pension and settled in Suffolk, where he lived in great style and, after buying the original Elveden Hall in 1863, redeveloped it in Indian style. Lord Iveagh built a new wing in the same shape and style as the Prince's house and connected the two with a great copper-domed central block.

ROTHSCHILD MANSIONS

In the late 19th and early 20th centuries, leading members of the Rothschild banking dynasty entertained lavishly in magnificent English country houses. Among these was Exbury in Hampshire, where Lionel de Rothschild built a Neoclassical house in the 1920s and created a superb 200 acre (80 ha)- woodland garden. Other Rothschild houses are Waddesdon Manor, Buckinghamshire, built in the style of a French chateau for Baron Ferdinand de Rothschild by the French architect, Gabriel Hippolyte Destailleur, in 1874–89, and Mentmore Towers, also in Buckinghamshire, built in a neo-Elizabethan style for Baron Meyer Amschel de Rothschild by Sir Joseph Paxton (former Chatsworth head gardener and designer of the Crystal Palace). Another was Ascott House, 3 miles (4.5km) from Mentmore Towers, built by Leopold de Rothschild in the 1870s.

Right: Baron Ferdinand de Rothschild filled Waddesdon Manor with artworks.

THE INDIAN HALL

Within the domed block was the Indian Hall, built on the basis of Indian durbar halls to designs by William Young with the advice of Sir Caspar Purdon Clarke, who was in charge of the Indian collection at the Victoria and Albert Museum in South Kensington, London.

Lord Iveagh spent £70,000 on the marble for this vast, dazzlingly white and intricately carved hall, which fills the full height of the domed section of the house. A special branch railway line was created from the nearest station, at Barnham, to bring the marble, stone and other materials to the site.

Left: Imperial grandeur – the superb Marble Hall at Elveden. In creating it, Lord Iveagh doubled the size of the existing hall.

Below: At Elveden Hall, Lord Iveagh hosted the grandest guests. King George V arrives for a shooting party in 1910.

Above: Entrance front at Polesden Lacey. In summer, vegetables and fruit grown on the 1,000 acre (400 ha)- estate were sent to Mrs Greville's London home each day.

Grandeur, however, was clearly more important than comfort: the hall had only two fireplaces and, despite under-floor central heating, was described by Elizabeth, Countess of Fingall, as 'England's coldest room'.

ROYAL SHOOTING PARTIES

Elvedon was especially renowned for its shooting; indeed, Lord Iveagh was first attracted to the estate because Prince Duleep Singh had developed it for game. Before Lord Iveagh's time, Edward VII, while still Prince of Wales, enjoyed shooting at Elveden in the company of Prince Duleep Singh; Lord Iveagh then hosted not only Edward VII but also George V and the future George VI for shooting parties on the estate.

POLESDEN LACEY

Another ostentatious Edwardian country house supported by brewing money was Polesden Lacey in Surrey: its owner, Margaret Greville, was the daughter of the Edinburgh brewer, Sir William McEwan. She entered English high society when, in 1901, she married Captain Ronald Greville, who through his friends the Keppels had access to

Edward VII. Margaret Greville became one of the leading hostesses of the day, welcoming politicians, ambassadors, foreign heads of state and the King himself to her lavish weekend parties.

The house at Polesden Lacey had once belonged to dramatist Richard Brinsley Sheridan in the 18th century, but became so dilapidated that it was entirely rebuilt by the great London builder Thomas Cubitt for Joseph Bonsor *c.*1835. The house was restructured and redecorated in 1902–5 by Ambrose Poynter for Sir Clinton Dawkins before it was bought by Sir William McEwan in 1906.

Employing the celebrated architects Charles Mewès and Arthur Davis (designers of the Ritz Hotel in London), Mrs Greville transformed the interior. Some of her rooms would have seemed overdone and even distasteful to a Victorian guest, but they were appreciated by the racy, sophisticated, 'modern' members of Edward VII's set. For example, she installed the reredos of a demolished Sir Christopher Wren church – St Matthew's, Friday Street, London – above the fireplace in her darkly panelled Hall; in her Drawing Room she fitted gilded panelling from an Italian palace and lines of tall mirrors. A second Drawing Room was provided for playing bridge.

A gentlemen's wing at Polesden Lacy included a Smoking Room, Billiard Room and Gun Room. There was also a Library and a fine Dining Room. The finest food was a necessary attraction when the gourmand Edward VII was among the guests, and Mrs Greville was famed for the quality of her 'table' and her French chef.

Below: The Drawing Room at Polesden Lacey had five pairs of French windows – when they were unshuttered, the room was a blaze of light on chandelier and gilding.

BUCKINGHAM PALACE
AND CLARENCE HOUSE: ROYAL REFURBISHMENT

Standing proudly at the end of The Mall in central London, Buckingham Palace is the Queen's official London residence and probably the most recognizable and celebrated royal building in Britain (see also page 52). Its balcony facing The Mall has been the setting for many iconic royal moments, such as the celebration of victory in 1945 by George VI and the royal family, including a teenage Princess Elizabeth (the future Queen Elizabeth II). However, before the start of the 20th century the palace was little used by the country's royals.

It was Queen Victoria who established Buckingham Palace, rather than St James's Palace nearby, as the monarch's official London residence. But she did not spend much time there, living with Prince Albert mainly at Windsor Castle when they were not in the country, and, after Albert's death, spending prolonged periods at Balmoral and Osborne House while dust sheets covered the fine furniture and lavishly decorated rooms at Buckingham Palace.

GLITTER AND GLAMOUR
Edward VII, however, had different ideas. He moved into the palace on his accession in 1901 from his previous London base, Marlborough House. He redecorated and refurnished the palace

Above: The base of the Victoria Memorial, which is at the east front of Buckingham Palace, contains 23,000 tons of marble.

in the year of his coronation, 1902, and restored glitter and glamour to court life. Unfortunately, his redecoration of the palace swept away many of the splendid Regency and early Victorian interiors, which were replaced by a rather uninspiring white and gold decorative scheme designed by C.H. Bessant.

IN MEMORY OF VICTORIA
The forecourt in front of the palace's east front was laid out at the beginning of George V's reign, in 1911. At the same time, the Victoria Memorial statue by Thomas Brock was set up before the palace on a great base of white marble, designed by Sir Aston Webb. The statue of Victoria faces towards The Mall, while

Left: While Edward VII certainly breathed new life into Buckingham Palace, historians regret that his redecoration (here of the King's private Sitting Room) was uninspiring.

on the other three sides are figures of the Angels of Justice and Truth and a personification of Charity. The golden figure on the pinnacle represents Victory.

The Admiralty Arch at the other end of The Mall, separating it from Trafalgar Square, was designed by Sir Aston Webb as part of the Victoria Memorial scheme and erected in 1910, a year earlier than the statue itself.

NEW EAST FRONT

In 1913, Sir Aston undertook the refacing of the east front of Buckingham Palace. When building the east front in 1847–50, Edward Blore had used a soft Caen stone, which had not weathered well in soot-laden London and so needed replacing; Sir Aston used a fine, grey Portland stone. His dignified east façade faces on to a gravelled forecourt enclosed by splendid ironwork gates and railings, providing a suitably grand public face for the palace. Webb created new gateposts but reused a number of older stone piers between the lengths of railing: among these are some, with floral swags and regal lions' heads, made in 1800 by Edward Wyatt for George III. The forecourt is the setting for the Changing of the Guard ceremony.

'GEORGIAN' REFURBISHMENT

In George V's reign, Queen Mary carried out a substantial refurbishment at the palace. She used what was then considered a 'Georgian' colour scheme of Chinese yellow, buff and celadon green. In 1914, the Picture Gallery was remodelled, and a new glazed ceiling installed to replace the work of Nash. Charles Allom decorated it using Chinese wallpapers and silk hangings that had been found in storage (and were probably

Above: A bedroom in the royal suite at Buckingham Palace in the time of Edward VII, who redecorated the palace interior.

originally intended by George IV for the Brighton Pavilion) to redecorate the Yellow Drawing Room and the Centre Room. Allom's work was much acclaimed and rewarded with a knighthood.

CLARENCE HOUSE

An elegant stuccoed building in Stable Yard Road, beside St James's Palace, Clarence House is the London residence of the Prince of Wales and Duchess of Cornwall. It was built by John Nash in 1825–7 for William, Duke of Clarence (the future William IV), who continued to live there while reigning as King in 1830–7.

The house has had a varied history within the royal family, having been the London home of William IV's unmarried sister, Princess Augusta, in 1837–40, then of Victoria's mother, the Duchess of Kent, in 1840–61. Subsequently it served as the official residence of Prince Alfred, Duke of Edinburgh, in 1866–1900: during these years, a Russian Orthodox chapel was installed on the first floor for use by Alfred's wife, Marie Alexandrovna, Duchess of Edinburgh, who was the daughter of Tsar Alexander II of Russia. In 1900–42, Arthur, the Duke of Connaught and third son of Queen Victoria, lived in the house. For the last three years of World War II,

Clarence House was the headquarters of the Red Cross and the St John's Ambulance Brigade.

Clarence House became the London home of Princess Elizabeth (the future Elizabeth II) and the Duke of Edinburgh on their marriage in 1947. Following

Above: The Drawing Room at Clarence House in 1981, when it was the London residence of Elizabeth, the Queen Mother.

Elizabeth's accession, Clarence House was the London residence of Queen Elizabeth, the Queen Mother, from 1953 to 2002.

MANDERSTON AND SENNOWE PARK
THE EDWARDIAN COUNTRY HOUSE

The 18th-century country house of Manderston at Duns, in Berwickshire, was lavishly rebuilt in 1901–5 by the architect John Kinross for Sir James Miller. A wealthy trader's son, Sir James had entered the top drawer of the British aristocracy in 1893 by marrying the Honourable Eveline Curzon, daughter of Lord Scarsdale. Lady Miller had grown up amid the splendour of the Robert Adam interiors at Kedleston Hall in Derbyshire, and Sir James wanted to keep his bride in the style to which she was accustomed. He told Kinross that money was no object in the redevelopment of Manderston. In the event, the house combined the elegance of Kedleston Hall with the convenience of the latest 20th-century inventions.

TRIBUTE TO KEDLESTON HALL
Kinross enlarged the main house, rebuilding the attic, as well as adding a basement, a service court and a new

Below: The Drawing Room at Manderston. The Millers' designers, Mellier and Co., used an opulent, French-influenced style.

west wing of gentlemen's rooms, including a gun room and bachelor bedrooms. He completely rebuilt the entrance front.

Much of the interior was a tribute to Kedleston Hall: in the Entrance Hall, the stuccoed fireplace and rounded patterning of inlaid floor marble are copies of those in the Marble Hall at Kedleston, while the Ballroom ceiling is derived from that of the Kedleston Dining Room. The lavish interior also

Above: The garden front at Manderston. The house combined elegance and tradition with all the latest modern conveniences.

features a Louis XVI-style staircase with a silvered balustrade, based on that of the Petit Trianon palace at Versailles. Kinross also took account of the requirements of modern comfort and style, including electric lighting and a 'motor house' containing a basement engineer's area.

SENNOWE PARK
Sennowe Park, at Guist in Norfolk, was designed by the Norwich architect, George Skipper, for Thomas Cook, grandson of the founder of the travel firm of that name, beginning in 1905. Skipper created a flamboyant mansion with a curved bay on the entrance front topped with standing figures. Within, the highly decorated staircase beneath an oval cupola and the vast fireplace with Grinling Gibbons-style carving in the grand 50ft (15m)- long Saloon added to the highly individual mix of styles. Elaborate stone carving throughout was done by Italian masons.

CASTLE DROGO
SIR EDWIN LUTYEN'S 20TH-CENTURY CASTLE

Celebrated as the last castle built in Britain, this imposing granite pile occupies a crag overlooking the River Teign gorge in Devon, with breathtaking views of Dartmoor. It was built in 1912–30 by Edwin Lutyens for Julius Charles Drew, who had made a great fortune importing Indian tea and establishing a chain of grocer shops.

Armed with a genealogy that suggested he was descended from a Norman knight named Drogo via the Drewe family of Drewsteignton, in Devon, Drew was determined to create a stone memorial to his wealth and his family's descent. He added an 'e' to his surname by deed poll and bought an estate in Drewsteignton. He then engaged the leading architect, Edwin Lutyens.

Drewe demanded a genuine stronghold, not a pastiche castle. The site was chosen in 1910. Over the next two decades, architect and client had

Below: Above the doorway is the Drewe lion and beneath it the family motto Drogo Nomen et Virtus Arma Dedit ('Drewe is the name and Valour gave it Arms').

many disagreements. Lutyens was often away setting out the new Indian capital of Delhi, and work proceeded under the supervision of Devon masons, Cleeve and Dewdney, and Clerk of Works, John Walker.

Below: As well as laying out Delhi and building many country houses, Lutyens designed the Cenotaph (London) and the British Embassy in Washington, D.C.

Above: Like a castle of old, Lutyens' building occupies the high ground, overlooking steep banks and a river far below.

A FORMIDABLE CASTLE

In the end, Lutyens and Walker created a formidable structure, with solid granite walls in places 6ft (1.8m) thick, austere façades, a turreted entrance with genuine portcullis, and a medieval-style interior with great expanses of granite and oak. Above the entrance door is a bas-relief of the Drewe lion by Herbert Palliser.

Drewe died in 1931, only a year after Drogo was completed; his grandson gave the castle to the National Trust in 1974.

ATTENTION TO DETAIL

The house combines a principal two-storey wing containing staterooms with a three-storey wing housing rooms for family and servants, both connected by a grand staircase. The Drawing Room and Dining Room are wood-panelled; the first contains large mullion windows and the second has an elaborate plaster-work ceiling. There is Edwardian luxury in the bathrooms. Lutyens attended to every feature of the design, down to the billiard table in the Billiard Room.

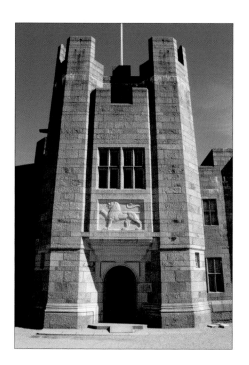

ELTHAM PALACE
THE COURTAULDS' ART DECO FANTASY

In 1931–6, Stephen and Virgina Courtauld built a splendid Art Deco house adjoining the historic remains of Eltham Palace in south-east London. At the same time, they undertook the restoration of the 15th-century Great Hall, built by Edward IV, and other parts of the palace, which was a boyhood haunt and great favourite of Henry VIII.

ART DECO STYLE

The Courtaulds commissioned John Seely and Paul Paget to build the new house and Peter Malacrida to decorate it. The sleek, elegant Art Deco style they used swept Europe and the United States in the wake of the 1925 Exposition Internationale des Arts Décoratifs et Industriels Modernes in Paris, from which it took its name. It used 'modern-looking', streamlined shapes often decorated with stylized or geometric ornament.

Below: The elegant Entrance Hall. After taking control of the house in the 1990s, English Heritage used period photos to restore the furnishings to their 1930s look.

Above: In the 1930s, Stephen and Virginia Courtauld remodelled the Tudor remains of Eltham Palace into an Art Deco house.

The Courtaulds' new house was built with all the most modern conveniences, such as underfloor heating and a sound system in all rooms. The interior was lavish: onyx and gold plate in the bathroom, an aluminium-foil ceiling in the Dining Room, veneered walls and elegant fitted furniture. The Entrance Hall was lit through a glazed concrete dome.

OLD-FASHIONED CLEANING

One way in which the new Eltham Palace was less than up-to-date was its use of a centralized vacuum cleaning system, which had been the latest thing at around the turn of the century, rather than the newest mobile vacuum cleaners. These centralized pumps had been used since *c.*1905, when one was fitted at Minterne Magna in Dorset.

NEW OWNERSHIP

The Courtaulds also redesigned the gardens at Eltham Palace, which contain the original moat and bridge. They lived at Eltham until 1944, when they moved to Scotland, and the Royal Army Education Corps took on the lease. In 1995, the palace and Art Deco house passed into the care of English Heritage, who carried out a painstaking restoration.

Below: The bathroom is lined with gold mosaic. A statue of the goddess Psyche looks down on the bath and its gold-plated taps.

PLAS NEWYDD AND PORT LYMPNE
REX WHISTLER AND THE MODERN COUNTRY HOUSE

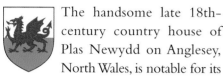

The handsome late 18th-century country house of Plas Newydd on Anglesey, North Wales, is notable for its architecture and situation as well as for its interior decoration. The house was built in 1793-9 by James Wyatt, architect of Heveningham Hall, Suffolk, and Fonthill Abbey, Wiltshire. It combines the Classical style with the Gothic for which Wyatt was celebrated. Situated overlooking the Menai Straits, the house has breathtaking views of Snowdonia.

REX WHISTLER

Whistler had made his name aged 22 in 1927, when still a student at the Slade School of Art in London, by creating a highly imaginative mural entitled *The Expedition in Pursuit of Rare Meats* in the Tea Rooms at the Tate Gallery. As well as painting society portraits and working in book illustration, theatre design and advertising, he continued throughout his short career to paint

Below: Whistler's extraordinary mural in the Dining Room at Plas Newydd is the largest of the artist's many wall paintings.

large-scale murals at country homes such as Plas Newydd, which is particularly celebrated for his 58ft (18m) mural of a romantic Italianate coastal landscape in the Dining Room, painted in 1936-7. It was commissioned by Plas Newydd's owner, Charles Paget, 6th Marquess of Anglesey, and while staying there Whistler fell in love with his daughter, Caroline, and made a number of rather whimsical references to his passion in the painting. In one part of the image,

Above: Herbert Baker drew on his experience building Cecil Rhodes's South African home in designing Port Lympne.

Lady Caroline (as Juliet) stands on a balcony while beneath stands the pining figure of Romeo (a self-portrait). Although apparently a mural, the painting is in fact a vast canvas.

Whistler's work inspired a vogue for ambitious country-house murals that lasted throughout the 20th century, but his career was cut short when he was killed, aged 39, during active service in World War II in July 1944. Earlier, at Mottisfont Abbey, a former priory turned country house in Hampshire, he painted, in 1938–9, an extraordinary *trompe l'oeil* Gothic Drawing Room that mimics intricate plasterwork in paint.

PORT LYMPNE

This handsome house in Kent was built for Sir Philip Sassoon, just before World War I, by the fashionable architect, Sir Herbert Baker, in the 'Dutch Colonial Style' used in South Africa. It was very highly regarded at the time, being described as 'the most remarkable modern house in England'. Here, Whistler created a widely admired 'tent room'.

THE 'GOLDEN TRIANGLE'
GATCOMBE , HIGHGROVE AND NETHER LYPIATT

Gloucestershire claims the name of 'the royal county' because there are three country houses owned by members of the Queen's family in the area. The three houses – Gatcombe Park near Minchinhampton, Highgrove House near Tetbury, and Nether Lypiatt Manor near Stroud – are known together as the royals' 'Golden Triangle'.

GATCOMBE PARK
The Queen bought Gatcombe Park, near Minchinhampton, for Princess Anne and her first husband, Captain Mark Phillips, as a belated wedding present in 1976.

Both keen riders, Princess Anne and Captain Phillips held the annual Gatcombe Park horse trials on the estate each August. After their marriage was dissolved in 1992, Princess Anne married Commander Timothy Laurence and the Princess and her family continued to hold the annual event.

Below: Highgrove House. The Prince of Wales's sheep graze on the lawn before the Georgian building. In the 1980s, the Prince added an open balustrade to the house.

Above: Gatcombe Park was built in the 1740s of Bath stone. The estate, venue for the horse trials, is of 730 acres (295ha).

Gatcombe Park was built in the 1740s by a local master mason, Francis Franklin, for Edward Sheppard; wings were added in the early 19th century by George Basevi, cousin of Disraeli and pupil of the architect, Sir John Soane. Later work included the addition of a conservatory in 1829. Its owners have included Samuel Courtauld and the Conservative minister 'RAB' Butler.

HIGHGROVE HOUSE
Purchased by the Duchy of Cornwall in 1980, Highgrove House was home to Prince Charles and Diana, Princess of

Wales, during the early years of their marriage. The three-storey five-bay Georgian building is rectangular with an originally columned portico (now glazed and enclosed) on the entrance front; within, there are four reception rooms. It was built in 1796–8 for a locally prominent Huguenot family named Paul. It originally stood in 350 acres (140ha), but the estate has been greatly enlarged by the Prince, who practises organic farming on the land. The Prince has also developed a fine walled garden on the Highgrove estate.

NETHER LYPIATT MANOR
Prince and Princess Michael of Kent bought Nether Lypiatt Manor in 1981. The house was built in 1698 by Judge Cox. It is said to be haunted by the ghost of the judge's son, who committed suicide in one of the rooms. Most of the main rooms are fitted with elegant beech, chestnut or oak panelling; there is a splendid original staircase. The house is faced in Cotswold stone.

Below: Nether Lypiatt. Apart from the fact that it has royal owners, the house is most celebrated for its 17th-century staircase.

BIRKHALL, MEY AND GLAMIS
SCOTLAND'S ROYAL RESIDENCES

The modern period has seen the restoration of several ancient buildings by members of the British royal family.

BIRKHALL

The relatively modest royal house of Birkhall stands on the edge of the Balmoral estate in Aberdeenshire, overlooking the River Muick. It is the Deeside residence of the Prince of Wales, where he spent a two-week honeymoon in 2005, following his marriage to the Duchess of Cornwall.

Birkhall was built in 1715. The house was bought by Queen Victoria and Prince Albert in 1849, the year after their first stay at Balmoral. It has been popular with many generations of their descendants, including the Duke and Duchess of York (the future George VI and Queen Elizabeth) in the 1930s; and by Princess Elizabeth (the future Queen Elizabeth II) and Prince Philip, the Duke of Edinburgh, in 1947–52; as well as Prince Charles. Queen Elizabeth, the Queen Mother, made it her Deeside residence in 1952–2002; she built a new wing containing six bedrooms in the 1950s and visited every spring. Prince Charles and the Duchess of Cornwall used the interior designer Robert Kine to redecorate the house.

Below: The Castle of Mey stands just 1,200ft (370m) from the sea, with views of Pentland Firth and the Orkney Islands.

THE CASTLE OF MEY

This castle in Caithness was restored by Queen Elizabeth, the Queen Mother, after she purchased it in 1952. The castle, a stone tower house built on a Z-plan by George, 4th Earl of Caithness, in 1566–72, was seriously dilapidated when the Queen saw and fell instantly in love with it in 1952, when she was mourning the death of her husband, King George VI. In a romantic position on the rugged Caithness coast, just 6 miles (9.5km) from John O'Groats and overlooking the Pentland Firth, it is Britain's most northerly castle. Its 2,000 acre (800 ha)- estate includes celebrated gardens. When purchased by the Queen in 1952, it was known as Barrogill Castle, but has since reverted to its ancient name, the Castle of Mey.

GLAMIS CASTLE

Queen Elizabeth, the Queen Mother, always had a strong emotional attachment to Scotland, having spent many childhood summers at her family's ancestral home, Glamis Castle in Tayside. The castle, famous above all as the setting for William Shakespeare's play *Macbeth*, was originally a royal

Above: The Sitting Room used by Queen Elizabeth, the Queen Mother, at Glamis Castle. With two bedrooms, it is part of a suite set aside for royal visitors at Glamis.

hunting lodge. It was transformed into a castle with an L-shaped keep in the early 15th century by the Queen Mother's ancestor, Sir John Lyon. In the Victorian era, the castle was modernized, with the introduction of gas and electricity; the east wing, in the Scottish Baronial style, was added in 1891. In 1930, the future Queen Mother gave birth to Princess Margaret there.

Below: In the words of the late Queen Elizabeth, the Queen Mother, Birkhall is 'a small big house, or a big small house'.

EILEAN DONAN AND CLANDON PARK
MAGNIFICENT RESTORATION

Beneath vast skies, on its own small island at the head of Loch Duich and looking towards Skye, Eilean Donan castle is perhaps the most spectacularly situated building in Britain. A castle has stood here since *c*.1220, but the building we see today is the product of a painstaking 20th-century rebuilding. For 20 years, beginning in 1912, Lt-Col. John MacRae-Gilstrap rebuilt the ruined castle that had been guarded by his MacRae ancestors in the 16th century.

Above: Strategic position. Eilean Donan Castle commands the waters of Loch Duich. On clear days, the Isle of Skye is plainly visible in the distance.

EARLY BEGINNINGS

The original castle had a long and romantic history. Its name refers to Abbot Donan, an Irish missionary to Scotland from Iona who reputedly built his hermitage on this spot during the early 600s. The first castle was built around 600 years later, in the reign of Alexander II, to defend this strategically important location against Danish and Norse incursions. Alexander III gave the fortress to Colin Fitzgerald, ancestor of clan MacKenzie, in 1263, as a reward for service at the Battle of Largs, in which the defeat of Norway won Scotland control of the Western Isles. Then, in 1306, Robert the Bruce was given refuge in the castle.

THE MACRAE PROTECTORS

In *c*.1360, the MacRaes entered the service of the MacKenzie clan as bodyguards, proving so effective that they became known as 'MacKenzies' Mail Shirt'. The MacRaes were appointed hereditary constables of Eilean Donan Castle in 1509, a position that brought with it significant rights of control and enforcement over the surrounding hotly contested region. They often came under attack – famously in 1539, when Donald MacRae and his garrison kept at bay an army of 400 under Donald Gorm, Lord of the Isles, and MacRae is said to have killed Gorm with his very last arrow.

NAVAL ONSLAUGHT

The castle was reduced to ruins by the might of the English Navy in 1719. William MacKenzie, 5th Earl of

---

HIDDEN GLORIES: RESTORING CLANDON PARK AND UPPARK

The National Trust has carried out a series of painstaking restorations of castles and country houses. Pride of place should, perhaps, go to its first major restoration project: Clandon Park, near Guildford in Surrey. The Palladian mansion – designed *c*.1730 by Italian architect Giacomo Leoni and set in 'Capability' Brown parkland – was given to the Trust in 1956. Over two years, the Trust spent around £200,000 restoring the house to its 18th-century prime.

Its magnificent Marble Hall features stucco work by the celebrated Italian craftsmen Arturi and Bagutti, which was skilfully finished to look like marble. Restorers discovered this delicate work beneath thick layers of whitewash.

The Trust's inspired and painstaking restoration of the 17th-century country house of Uppark, West Sussex, in the 1990s, combined the latest scientific techniques with a revival of a number of historic crafts. The project was made necessary by a devastating fire that struck on 30 August 1989. The Trust's craftsmen and -women restored Uppark – which, prior to the fire, was celebrated as one of England's best-preserved houses – to quite superb condition.

Left: Clandon Park was given the kind of meticulous restoration appropriate for one of England's finest Palladian mansions.

Above: Eilean Donan Castle's colourful past and beautiful situation – and the romance associated with its restoration – explain its great appeal as a subject for photographs.

Seaforth, was a supporter of the Jacobite cause (the movement to restore the House of Stuart to the throne) and garrisoned Eilean Donan with a small group of Spanish troops sent to lead an uprising. Three English warships bombarded the fortress until it was a mere ruin. Meanwhile, because a Spanish support fleet failed to arrive, the 1719 uprising petered out in a low-key defeat of a small force of Spaniards and high-landers at Glenshiel by a royalist army from Inverness.

RETURN TO GLORY

Eilean Donan remained an evocative ruin for almost two centuries until a 20th-century MacRae set out to honour his ancestors' memory by restoring the castle to its former glory. Even the restoration has a romantic tale attached to it. Because the castle was so badly ruined, the restorers could not be sure what it had looked like, but a clan descendant named Farquhar MacRae had a vision in a dream of the castle as

it once was, and worked with the castle's new owner to make the vision a reality. Then, when restoration was nearing completion, plans of the castle dated to 1714 were found in Edinburgh; curiously, they matched the details of the vision in remarkable detail.

THE CASTLE TODAY

A stone causeway leads from the main-land across the loch to the island. A portcullis guards the entrance in the outer walls; above the entrance is a Gaelic inscription that translates: 'If a MacRae is inside, there will never be a Fraser outside.' This refers to an alliance between the clans that dates back to the 14th century, when the MacRaes fos-tered a young heiress who later married into the Frasers. On the gate of Beaufort Castle, she raised a similar inscription, in Gaelic: 'If a Fraser resides within, no MacRaes will be left without.'

Within, across a walled courtyard, stands the three-storey main tower of the castle. In its barrel-vaulted basement, which has walls 14ft (4m) thick, is the Billeting Room, hung with pictures of the MacRaes in battle, at Sheriffmuir in 1715 and Glenshiel in 1719. Above is the Banqueting Hall, with an oak-timbered

ceiling, a circular wrought-iron chandelier and splendid chimney-piece. The hall also contains a portrait of Lt-Col. John MacRae-Gilstrap, the castle's rebuilder, and a broadsword connected to his ancestor John MacRae, dubbed 'the Bard of Kintail', who fought at the Battle of Culloden in 1746 and then in the American War of Independence. On the floors above are sleeping chambers, accessed via a stair-case turret. From the battlements stretch magnificent views of three lochs: Alsh, Long and Duich.

Below: A stone roadway connects the castle on the 'Isle of Donan' to the mainland. It was added as part of the restoration work.

NEO-PALLADIAN COUNTRY HOUSES
ARUNDEL PARK, KINGS WALDEN BURY, WAVERTON AND NEWFIELD

Waverton House in Gloucestershire and Newfield in North Yorkshire are fine examples of the Neo-Palladian country house that has been widely popular since the mid-20th century. Both houses were designed by architect Quinlan Terry, the first in 1977 for Jocelyn Hambro of the Hambro banking family, and the second in 1980 for carpet magnate Michael Abrahams. Although some country house patrons have chosen to build in the Modern style (see below), most have chosen neo-Palladian or neo-Georgian architecture for its emphasis on continuity and tradition – and perhaps also from a desire to celebrate England's heritage.

ARUNDEL PARK

The revival of Palladian designs began at Arundel Park, Sussex, in the 1950s. The Duchess of Norfolk became unhappy with the lack of privacy resulting from the opening of Arundel Castle to the public, and persuaded her husband to build a new house in a more secluded spot in the grounds. Architect Claud Phillimore built the house in 1958–62 on Neo-Palladian lines, with a central block linked to two side pavilions. (This design was in fact the Duchess's own idea; she is said to have been inspired by a visit to Ditchley Park in Oxfordshire.)

Arundel Park's handsome main block contains a Dining Room and Drawing Room along the garden front and a grand, top-lit Staircase Hall filling the whole height of the house beneath a vaulted ceiling. The interior harmonizes with the 18th-century elegance of the exterior: Phillimore designed double doors that are a copy of those in the Double Cube Room at Wilton

THE MODERN STYLE IN COUNTRY HOUSES

Eaton Hall in Cheshire was once the most notable modern country house. It was built in 1971–3 for Robert Grosvenor, 5th Duke of Westminster, to designs by John Dennys on the site of an imposing but largely demolished Victorian house at Eaton. Dennys's angular design caused a major controversy and was likened by the Duke of Bedford to a factory office block on a bypass. But in 1989 work began to encase it in a more traditional facing believed to blend more happily with the countryside.

Stratton Park in Hampshire is among the most prominent of the country houses built in the later 20th century in the Modern style. Constructed in 1963–5 by Stephen Gardiner and Christopher Knight, it stands alongside a vast Doric

portico – all that remains of a 19th-century Greek Revival mansion built by George Dance the Younger. The L-shaped house contains the main family rooms in a wing (the long arm of the L) running parallel with the portico, while at right angles a conservatory and pond link to the

Left: John Dennys's angular design for Eaton Hall was the subject of controversy and the building was refaced in 1989.

Above: The white block of Eaton Hall stood a little incongruously at the centre of a very grand estate – with formal gardens on one side and an avenue on the other.

evocative classical remains of the portico. Another substantial Modern country house is Witley Park, Surrey, built by Patrick Gwynne in 1961–2. Its two wings are hexagonal, its interior filled with gadgetry.

House and imported antique marble chimney-pieces. Interior decorator, John Fowler, supervised the colours and decorative details.

KINGS WALDEN BURY

Arundel Park's three-part neo-Palladian design was highly influential, as was a house in a similar style – built by Quinlan Terry with his then partner, Raymond Erith, at Kings Walden Bury in Hertfordshire, in 1967–71. The patron, Sir Thomas Milburne-Swinnerton-Pilkington, wanted to replace the 1890s house on the site with a new and elegant mansion.

Erith and Terry, outspoken critics of the Modern movement in architecture and ardent promoters of Classicism, produced a handsome and substantial house in Italian-Palladian style, with a columned and pedimented entrance front with 'Venetian windows', leading into a large hall with a stone floor and a barrel-vaulted staircase. The four principal rooms are the Drawing Room, Sitting Room, Dining Room and Kitchen.

Below: Quinlan Terry used classic Palladian proportions at Waverton House. The doorcase on the entrance front has Ionic supports.

WAVERTON HOUSE

Kings Walden Bury proved to be a prototype for country houses in the last decades of the 20th century. At Waverton, Gloucestershire, Terry again used the design of a central block and side pavilions. The large, seven-bedroom main house has a grand Staircase Hall, featuring a central staircase lit from above. The Drawing Room, Kitchen, Study and Dining Room are on the ground floor. Staff quarters and service rooms are in the long side wings. Terry made good use of local materials (on the insistence of the local planners): the roof has flags of Cotswold stone, while the walls are faced in stone from demolished local barns.

Above: Newfield was designed as a working house at the centre of a farm. A substantial forecourt extends before it, just as in Palladio's villas in the Veneto.

NEWFIELD

At Newfield in North Yorkshire, Quinlan Terry reworked the designs of his patron, Michael Abrahams – who had himself studied Palladio. The house they produced between them consists of a handsome central block, containing the Drawing Room, Hall and Dining Room with kitchen, with small side wings for staff and necessary service spaces. As at Waverton House, it is built of local stone.

A CLASSICAL FUTURE?

The preference for Neo-Palladian and other English classical styles in country house architecture has remained strong in the early years of the 21st century. In 2001–3, Quinlan Terry worked with his son, Francis, in the creation of the country house of Ferne Park, Dorset: its entrance is adorned with four large columns and a pediment and leads into a square hall with Doric columns. It is built in Portland and Chilmark stone.

Another design by Quinlan Terry, at Juniper Hill in Buckinghamshire in 1999-2002, features a large Ionic portico on its main entrance that strongly recalls the first English Palladian houses, such as Colen Campbell's Stourhead House, Wiltshire.

GLOSSARY

architrave Part of the entablature (upper part) of a classical order. The architrave is the lintel (horizontal beam) directly above the top of the column and beneath the frieze. Also the moulded pane of a window or door.

bailey Area enclosed by the walls of a castle; also called 'ward'. Compare motte, the mound on which the keep was built. The most common early Norman castles consisted of a motte (with an, initially, wooden and, later, stone tower) and a bailey enclosed by an earthwork wall topped with a palisade.

barbican Heavily fortified defensive structure, often a double tower, usually built out from the castle gateway.

Baronial Style of Scottish architecture, employed only rarely in England, in vogue from the early 1800s until *c.*1920. The Baronial style used towers with small turrets, stepped gables and crenellations to create the appearance of a 'fairytale castle', such as Balmoral Castle.

Baroque Sensuous and dramatic style in art and architecture, originating in Rome around 1600, that found expression in highly ornamented, monumental buildings set in grand, landscaped parks. English Baroque buildings in *c.*1700–30 are characterized by their dramatic use of space and movement, surface ornamentation and dynamic interaction with their setting. Great examples include Castle Howard and Blenheim Palace.

basilica In ancient Roman buildings, a big public hall.

bastide Walled town built alongside a castle. Originally, a French term, but applied to castle-town developments, such as Conwy in Wales.

bastion Projecting fortification on the curtain wall of a castle.

battlements Low defensive wall or parapet on the top of a castle's curtain wall or its towers, with indented sections (*embrasures* or *crenelles*) and raised parts (*merlons* or *cops*). Battlements were later

Above: Detail of the Tuscan Temple at Rievaulx Terrace showing the entablature.

used for decoration to give homes the appearance of a castle.

bay Section of a house's outer wall, defined by vertical features, such as windows, columns and pilasters.

belvedere Raised building or room that commands a fine view.

burgh Anglo-Saxon fortified town.

chinoiserie Originally, French term for interior decoration that mimicked Chinese arts and colour schemes. Starting in the 17th century, chinoiserie remained in vogue until the 19th century.

classical Style in English architecture pioneered by Inigo Jones in the 17th century, inspired by buildings of ancient Greece and Rome and Italian Renaissance interpretations of them. Fine examples of Jones's classical architecture in England include the Queen's House, Greenwich, and the Banqueting Hall, Whitehall. *See also* Palladian.

corbel Projecting bracket in a wall supporting a vault or beam.

cornice Part of the entablature (upper part) of a classical order, consisting of a moulded decoration set horizontally above the frieze. Also (more generally) the moulding between wall and ceiling.

course Continuous line or layer of stones or bricks in a wall.

cupola Dome.

curtain wall A castle's outer wall, linking its towers.

drawbridge Movable bridge across the castle moat. Drawbridges could be moved horizontally or lifted vertically.

dressed stone Trimmed, smoothed and neatly cut stone.

eave Part of a sloping roof that projects over the top of the wall.

English bond In brickwork, the alternating use along a course of the brick ends ('headers') and the brick sides ('stretchers'). *See also* Flemish bond.

entablature The part of the classical order that is above a wall or column. Includes the architrave, the frieze and the cornice.

façade One of the main exteriors of a building, usually containing an entrance.

facing Layer of one material laid over another.

Flemish bond In brickwork, the use of the brick ends ('headers') throughout one course and then the brick sides ('stretchers') throughout the next. *See also* English bond.

fluting Vertical series of grooves cut on classical columns etc. *See also* orders.

frieze Part of the entablature of a classical order, found above the architrave and consisting of decorative sculpted or painted decoration. Also used more generally for a continuous strip of decoration around the upper walls of a room.

gable Triangular profile at the end of a gable-roof (one with two sloping sides). Sometimes, also, a triangular extension above a doorway.

garderobe In castles and medieval houses, a privy or toilet. Alternatively, a walk-in wardrobe.

Gothic Series of styles in medieval architecture *c.*1150–*c.*1500. In England, it applied principally to ecclesiastical architecture: there were no castles or fortified manor houses built in the Gothic style.

Great Hall Main room in the castle or medieval house, used up to Tudor times for dining and social occasions.

ha-ha Sunken ditch creating a hidden boundary between gardens and parkland in a country estate. Invented in the 18th century, it was invisible from the house and was reputedly named after the expression of surprise ('Ha! Ha!') uttered when a visitor chanced upon it. It kept grazing parkland animals out of the gardens.

hammer-beam roof One in which the roof arch is supported by short beams set into the wall at the base of the roof.

keep Most strongly fortified part of a castle, usually containing the lord's apartments and often called the *donjon* (French for 'lordship'). It functioned as a stronghold within the castle to which defenders could retreat if the outer bailey were captured by besiegers. The keep was usually a stone tower standing on the motte, when there was one.

linen-fold panelling Tudor decorative carving of wood, which was made to look like folded linen. An example is the linen-fold panelling screen in the Great Hall at Compton Wynyates.

Long Gallery Feature of Tudor and especially Elizabethan-Jacobean houses, a long room was used as a promenade in bad weather and to display portraits and sculptures.

machicolation Section projecting from the outer face of a castle's curtain wall, with holes in the floor through which the defenders dropped missiles. Strictly, the machicolations were the actual holes.

mathematical tiles Tiles that resemble brick or stone. Used, for example, by Henry Holland to reface Althorp *c.*1790. Brick taxes around this time boosted the popularity of tiles as an alternative to bricks.

moat Man-made ditch surrounding a castle or town walls, usually full of water.

motte Mound on which the keep of a castle was built. *See also* bailey.

mullion Vertical divider in a window containing more than one pane of glass (light). *See also* transom.

obelisk Tall square column tapering to a pyramidal tip. Obelisks were often raised among temples and other garden buildings in the carefully planned parklands of Baroque and Palladian houses.

orders Column types in ancient Greek and Roman architecture, used in classical, Palladian and Greek Revival English buildings. There are five types: the plain and unornamented Tuscan; Doric, which has triglyphs (channelled blocks) along the frieze; Ionic, which has decoration like a scroll of parchment in the capital (the head of the column); Corinthian, which has decoration representing acanthus leaves on the capital; and Composite, which combines scroll and leaf decoration.

oriel window Projecting window supported by stone brackets or corbels.

Palladian 18th-century development of the classical style in architecture, named after and inspired by the works of the great Italian Renaissance architect Andrea Palladio (1508–80). Holkham Hall and Mereworth Castle are good examples of Palladian country houses.

pediment Raised triangular feature above a portico, door or window. It derived from the triangular gable ends of Greek temples with pitched roofs.

piano nobile Derived from the Italian *palazzo*, the first-floor level containing the main rooms in a classical building.

pilaster Flattened column used for decorative effect on a façade. A pilaster follows the rules of the classical orders.

portcullis Grill of wood or iron lowered for added defensive strength over a castle gateway.

portico Porch with roof and often pediment supported by columns.

Left: The greatest example of the Gothic Revival is the Palace of Westminster.

Above: Cupola and details of the roof at Castle Howard.

postern Small, secondary gate (often concealed) in castle or town walls. Members of the garrison could use the postern to make inconspicuous exits and entries or to launch a surprise attack on a besieging force.

revetment Retaining wall of masonry etc supporting the face of an earthen rampart or ditch.

Revival Use by patrons and architects of elements from an earlier architectural style. Examples include the late 18th-century/early 19th-century Greek Revival, and the several allied Victorian movements, such as the Norman, Tudor, Elizabethan and 'Jacobethan' Revivals.

rusticated Stone blocks that have been dressed roughly to suggest strength.

scroll Decorative moulding in the shape of an S.

shingles Wood pieces used in place of tiles.

solar Private chamber, usually on the first floor of a medieval–Tudor house, to which the lord's family could retreat from the public Great Hall. So called because it was fitted with large windows to allow in as much sunlight as possible.

spandrel Triangular space between an arch and a wall or between two arches.

squints hidden openings in a wall.

strapwork Late 16th- and early 17th-century style in ornament, making use of interlaced leather-like bands.

transom Horizontal divider in a window containing more than one pane of glass (light). *See also* mullion.

PROPERTY LISTINGS

All information was accurate at the time of going to press. Please note that many of these properties are not open to the public or are open for only a few days a year, and check with the property before visiting.

ALNWICK CASTLE
Alnwick, Northumberland
NE66 1NQ
01665 510777
www.alnwickcastle.com

ALTHORP
Althorp
Northampton NN7 4HQ
01604 770107
www.althorp.com

ANTONY HOUSE
Torpoint
Cornwall PL11 2QA
01752 812191
www.nationaltrust.org.uk

ARBURY HALL
Nuneaton
Warwickshire CV10 7PT
02476 382804
www.information-britain.co.uk

THE ARGORY
144 Derrycaw Road
Moy, Dungannon
Co. Armagh BT71 6NA
028 8778 4753
www.nationaltrust.org.uk

ARLINGTON COURT
Arlington, nr Barnstaple
Devon EX31 4LP
01271 850296
www.nationaltrust.org.uk

ARUNDEL CASTLE
Arundel
West Sussex BN18 9AB
01903 883136
www.arundelcastle.org.uk

BALMORAL CASTLE
Balmoral, Ballater, Aberdeenshire AB35 5TB
013397 42534
www.balmoralcastle.com

BEAULIEU
Brockenhurst, Hampshire SO42 7ZN
01590 612345
www.beaulieu.co.uk

BELFAST CASTLE
Antrim Road, Belfast BT15 5GR
028 9077 6925
www.belfastcastle.co.uk

BELSAY HALL
Belsay, near Ponteland
Northumberland NE20 0DX
01661 881636
www.english-heritage.org.uk

BIRKHALL
www.princeofwales.gov.uk/personalpro
files/residences/birkhall/

BLENHEIM PALACE
Woodstock Oxfordshire OX20 1PX
08700 602080
www.blenheimpalace.com

BLICKLING HALL
Blickling, Norwich, Norfolk NR11 6NF
01263 738030
www.nationaltrust.org.uk

BRIGHTON PAVILION
see **ROYAL PAVILION, THE**

BRODSWORTH HALL
Brodsworth, near Doncaster
South Yorkshire DN5 7XJ
01302 722598
www.english-heritage.org.uk

BUCKINGHAM PALACE
London SW1A 1AA
0202 7766 7300
www.royalcollection.org.uk

Above: Marlborough House.

CARDIFF CASTLE
Castle Street, Cardiff CF10 3RB
029 2087 8100
www.cardiffcastle.com

CARISBROOKE CASTLE
Newport, Isle of Wight PO30 1XY
01983 522107
www.english-heritage.org.uk

CARLTON TOWERS
Carlton, North Yorkshire, DN14 9LZ
01405 861 662
www.carltontowers.co.uk

CASTELL COCH
Tongwynlais, Cardiff CF4 7JS
029 2081 0101
www.cadw.wales.gov.uk

CASTLE COOLE
Enniskillen, Co Fermanagh BT74 6JY
028 6632 2690
www.nationaltrust.org.uk

CASTLE DROGO
Drewsteignton, Exeter EX6 6PB
01647 433306
www.nationaltrust.org.uk

CASTLE HOWARD
York, North Yorkshire YO60 7DA
01653 648444
www.castlehoward.co.uk

CASTLE OF MEY
Thurso, Caithness KW14 8XH
01847 851473
www.castleofmey.org.uk

CAWDOR CASTLE
Nairn IV12 5RD
01667 404401
www.cawdorcastle.com

CHATSWORTH
Bakewell, Derbyshire DE45 1PP
01246 565300
www.chatsworth.org

CHISWICK HOUSE
Burlington Lane
London W4 2RP
020 8995 0508
www.english-heritage.org.uk

CLANDON PARK
West Clandon, Guildford,
Surrey GU4 7RQ
01483 222482
www.nationaltrust.org.uk

CLARENCE HOUSE
www.princeofwales.gov.uk/personal
profiles/residences/clarencehouse

CLIVEDEN
Taplow, Maidenhead
Buckinghamshire SL6 0JA
01628 605069
www.nationaltrust.org.uk

CRESSELLY HOUSE
Pembrokeshire
Fax. 01646 687045
www.cresselly.com

CRONKHILL
Atcham, Shrewsbury
Shropshire SY5 6JP
01743 708123
www.nationaltrust.org.uk

CULZEAN CASTLE
Maybole KA19 8LE
0844 4932149
www.nts.org.uk

DITCHLEY PARK
Enstone, Oxfordshire OX7 4ER
01608 677346
www.ditchley.co.uk

EASTNOR CASTLE
near Ledbury, Herefordshire HR8 1RL
01531 633160
www.eastnorcastle.com

EATON HALL
Eaton Estate Office, Eccleston
Chester CH4 9ET
01244 684 400
www.eatonestate.co.uk

EILEAN DONAN CASTLE
Dornie, Kyle of Localsh,
Wester Ross IV40 8DX
01599 555202
www.eileandonancastle.com

ELTHAM PALACE
Court Yard, Eltham, London SE9 5QE
020 8294 2548
www.english-heritage.org.uk

ELVEDEN HALL
www.literarynorfolk.co.uk/elveden_hall.htm

FALKLAND PALACE
Falkland KY15 7BU
0844 4932186
www.nts.org.uk

FROGMORE HOUSE AND MAUSOLEUM
Windsor, Berkshire SL4 2HT
020 7766 7321
http://www.royalcollection.org.uk

GLAMIS CASTLE
Glamis by Forfar, Angus DD8 1RJ
01307 840393
www.glamis-castle.co.uk

GOODWOOD HOUSE
Goodwood, Chichester, West Sussex
PO18 0PX
01243 755048
www.goodwood.co.uk

Right: Queen Charlotte's Cottage, Kew.

GOSFORD CASTLE
Markethill, Armagh
County Armagh BT60 1FP
www.gosfordcastle.net

THE GRANGE
Northington Grange
New Alresford SO24 9TG
01962 868600
www.english-heritage.org.uk

GREAT PAGODA, KEW
Royal Botanic Gardens, Kew
Richmond, Surrey TW9 3AB
020 8332 5000
www.kew.orgl

HAREWOOD HOUSE
Harewood, Leeds,
West Yorkshire LS17 9LG
0113 2181010
www.harewood.org

HEATON HALL
Heaton Park
Manchester M25 5SW
0161 773 1231
www.manchestergalleries.org/html/
heaton/heaton_home.jsp

HEVENINGHAM HALL
Heveningham, Halesworth
Suffolk IP19 0PN
http://www.peerage.org/genealogy/heve
ningham.htm

HIGHCLERE CASTLE
Newbury
Berkshire RG20 9RN
01635 253210
www.highclerecastle.co.uk

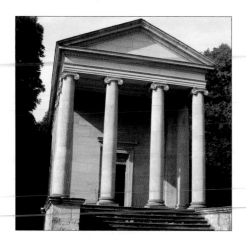

Above: The Ionic Temple, Rievaulx Terrace.

HIGHGROVE HOUSE
www.princeofwales.gov.uk/
personalprofiles/residences/highgrove/

HOLKHAM HALL
Wells-next-the-Sea
Norfolk NR23 1AB
01328 710227
www.holkham.co.uk

HOLYROODHOUSE PALACE
Canongate, The Royal Mile
Edinburgh EH8 8DX
0131 556 5100
www.royalcollection.org.uk

HOUGHTON HALL
Houghton, King's Lynn
Norfolk PE31 6UE
01485 528569
www.houghtonhall.com

HUGHENDEN MANOR
High Wycombe HP14 4LA
01494 755573
www.nationaltrust.org.uk

INVERARAY CASTLE
Inveraray
Argyll PA32 8XE
01499 302203
www.inveraray-castle.com

KEDLESTON HALL
Derby DE22 5JH
01332 842191
www.nationaltrust.org.uk

KENWOOD HOUSE
Hampstead Lane
London NW3 7JR
020 8348 1286
www.english-heritage.org.uk

KEW PALACE
Kew Gardens
Kew, Richmond
Surrey TW9 3AB
020 8332 5655
www.hrp.org.uk

KISIMUL CASTLE
Castlebay
Isle of Barra HS9 5UZ
01871 810 313
www.historic-scotland.gov.uk

KNEBWORTH HOUSE
Knebworth
Hertfordshire SG3 6PY
01438 812661
www.knebworthhouse.com

LONGFORD PARK
Stretford
Trafford: Edge Lane
Mancheter M32 8PX
0161 865 6030
www.friendsoflongfordpark.org.uk

LONGLEAT HOUSE
Longleat
Warminster
Wiltshire BA12 7NW
01985 844400
www.longleat.co.uk

LOSELEY PARK
Guildford
Surrey GU3 1HS
01483 304440
www.loseley-park.com

MANDERSTON
Duns
Berwickshire TD11 3PP
01361 882636
www.manderston.co.uk

Right: Castle Howard.

MARLBOROUGH HOUSE
Pall Mall
London SW1Y 5HX
020 77476500
www.thecommonwealth.org

MARBLE HILL HOUSE
Richmond Road
Twickenham TW1 2NL
020 8892 5115
www.english-heritage.org.uk

MELDON PARK
Morpeth, Northumberland
NE61 3SW
www.meldonpark.co.uk

MUNCASTER CASTLE
Ravenglass
Cumbria CA18 1RQ
01229 717614
www.muncaster.co.uk

NARROW WATER CASTLE
Warrenpoint, County Down
Northern Ireland BT34 3LE
028 4175 4262
www.narrowwatercastle.com

OSBORNE HOUSE
Osborne House, Royal Apartments,
East Cowes, Isle of Wight PO32 6JY
01983 200022
www.english-heritage.org.uk

OSTERLEY PARK
Jersey Road, Isleworth, Middlesex
TW7 4RB
020 8232 5050
www.nationaltrust.org.uk

PALACE OF WESTMINSTER
London SW1A 0AA
020 7219 3000
www.parliament.uk/parliament/guide/
palace.htm

PENRHYN CASTLE
Bangor LL57 4HN
01248 353084
www.nationaltrust.org.uk

PETWORTH HOUSE
Petworth, West Sussex GU28 0AE
01798 342207
www.nationaltrust.org.uk

PEVERIL CASTLE
Market Place, Castleton, Hope Valley
Derbyshire S33 8WQ
01433 620613
www.english-heritage.org.uk

PICTON CASTLE
Haverfordwest
Pembrokeshire
SA62 4AS
01437 751326
www.pictoncastle.co.uk

PLAS NEWYDD
Llanfairpwll, Anglesey LL61 6DQ
01248 715272
www.nationaltrust.org.uk

POLESDEN LACEY
Great Bookham, near Dorking
Surrey RH5 6BD
01372 452048
www.nationaltrust.org.uk

PORT LYMPNE
Port Lympne Wild Animal Park, Lympne,
Nr Hythe
Kent CT21 4PD
01303 234 111
www.totallywild.net/portlympne

PRIOR PARK LANDSCAPE GARDEN
Ralph Allen Drive
Bath BA2 5AH
01225 833422
www.nationaltrust.org.uk

QUEEN CHARLOTTE'S COTTAGE
Kew Palace, Royal Botanic Gardens Kew
Richmond, Surrey TW9 3AB
0844 482 7777
www.hrp.org.uk

RIEVAULX TERRACE AND TEMPLES
Rievaulx, Helmsley
North Yorkshire YO62 5LJ
01439 798340
www.nationaltrust.org.uk

ROUSHAM HOUSE
near Steeple Aston, Bicester
Oxfordshire OX25 4QX
01869 347110
www.rousham.org

THE ROYAL PAVILION
Brighton, East Sussex BN1 1EE
01273 290900
www.royalpavilion.org.uk

ST JAMES'S PALACE
1 Marlborough Road, London, SW1A
www.royal.gov.uk/TheRoyalResidences/
StJamessPalace/History.aspx

SANDRINGHAM HOUSE
Sandringham, Norfolk PE35 6EN
01553 612908
www.sandringham-estate.co.uk

SENNOWE PARK
Guist, Norfolk NR20 5PB
www.sennowepark.com

STOURHEAD HOUSE
near Warminster BA12 6QD
01747 841152
www.nationaltrust.org.uk

STOWE HOUSE
Contact Visitor Services Manager,
Stowe School, Buckingham MK18 5EH
01280 818229
www.shpt.org

STOWE LANDSCAPE GARDENS
near Buckingham MK18 5EH
01280 822850
www.nationaltrust.org.uk

Above: The Upper Ward, Windsor Castle.

STRAWBERRY HILL
St Mary's, Strawberry Hill,
Waldegrave Road
Twickenham TW1 4SX
020 8240 4224
www.friendsofstrawberryhill.org

SYON HOUSE
Syon Park
Brentford TW8 8JF
020 8560 0882
www.syonpark.co.uk

UPPARK
South Harting
Petersfield GU31 5QR
01730 825415
www.nationaltrust.org.uk

THE VYNE
Sherborne St John
Basingstoke RG24 9HL
01256 883858
www.nationaltrust.org.uk

WADDESDON MANOR
Waddeson, near Aylesbury,
Buckinghamshire HP18 0JH
01296 653226
www.waddesdon.org.uk

WINDSOR CASTLE
Windsor, Berkshire
SL4 1NJ
020 7766 7304
www.windsor.gov.uk or
www.royalcollection.org.uk

INDEX

  # ACKNOWLEDGEMENTS

Alamy: AA World Travel Library: 54b; Keith Allan: 8–9; Alastair Balderstone: 24b; Peter Barritt: 69br; Pat Behnk: 64bl; Bildarchiv Monheim GmbH: 7b, 31t, 34–5, 36t, 36bl, 37t, 37b; BL Images Ltd: 7t, 50t; Michael Booth: 60b, 80bl; Brinkstock: 65bl; Ros Drinkwater: 69t; Rod Edwards: 28bl; Mary Evans Picture Library: 51b; eye35.com: 50b; Tim Graham: 56t, 56b; Greenshoots Communications: 67b; John Henshall: 62t; Holmes Garden Photos: 28t; Imagebroker: 16–17; ISP Photography: 81tr; David Kilpatrick: 55b; Ian Leonard: 10tr, 55t, 79tc; Nick Lewis Photography: 54tr; The Marsden Archive: 70tr; Neil McAllister: 21b; Jeff Morgan: 66t; Eric Nathan: 53tr; David Newham: 71bl; PCL: 68b; John Peter Photography: 83bl; Popperfoto: 74b; Ben Ramos: 30b; Rob Rayworth: 89; Rolf Richardson: 48tr; Ruleofthirds: 84t; Ian Shaw: 57t; Shenval: 12; Simmons Aerofilms Ltd: 79b; Skyscan Photolibrary: 13t, 24t, 63t, 67tl; Homer Sykes: 86bl; John Taylor: 64t; Travelshots.com: 69bl; V&A Images: 27b; David Wootton: 71t;

The Art Archive: 22bl; Dagli Orti: 53tl; Jarrold Publishing: 13c, 13b, 31b, 45t, 68t, 84b; Private Collection MD: 76b, 77t, 71br; Private Collection/ Eileen Tweedy: 27tr;

The Bridgeman Archive: © Ashmolean Museum, University of Oxford: 44t; Cardiff Castle, Cardiff, Wales: 67b; Chiswick House, London: 23c, 25t; Kedleston Hall, Derbyshire: 42t, 42b, 43b; Kenwood House, London: 43t; Osterley Park, Middlesex: 6t; Plas Newydd, Anglesey: 81bl; Stourhead, Wiltshire: 22t;

Syon House, Middlesex: 40bl; Blenheim Palace, Oxfordshire: 20t; © Bonhams, London/Private Collection: 36br; © Burghley House Collection: 33bl; © Christie's Images/Private Collection: 62br; © City of Westminster Archive Centre, London: 20b; Eastnor Castle, Herefordshire: 51t, 65t; Giraudon, Bibliotheque Nationale, Paris, France: 70tl; © Guildhall Art Gallery, City of London: 52; Heveningham Hall, Suffolk: 44bl; Kew Gardens, London: 38t; Knebworth House, Hertfordshire: 70b; © Leeds Museums and Art Galleries (Temple Newsam House): 27tl; John Martin Robinson: 87b, 87t; © Philip Mould, Historical Portraits Ltd, London/ Private Collection: 28br; National Trust Photographic Library/Patrick Prendergast, Castle Coole, County Fermanagh, Northern Ireland: 45bl; Petworth House, Sussex /National Trust Photographic Library/Rupert Truman: 33br; Philadelphia Museum of Art, Pennsylvania, PA, USA: 23br; Polesden Lacey, Great Bookham, Surrey: 75b; Private Collection: 25b, 49t, 49b; Rousham House, Oxfordshire: 30t; Scottish National

Portrait Gallery, Edinburgh, Scotland: 41br; The Stapleton Collection, Private Collection: 26t, 29tr, 39t, 40br, 40t, 52t, 57b; © Christopher Wood Gallery, London, Private Collection: 19; © Yale Center for British Art, Paul Mellon Collection, USA: 38b, 44br

Corbis: Bettmann: 53b, 79bm; Angelo Hornak: 29tl; Massimo Listri: 49b; Adam Woolfitt: 86br

Darryl Curcher, Pennington PR: 58–9, 65br

Mary Evans Picture Library: 26b, 54tc

Tim Graham Picture Library: 46t, 46b, 47t, 76t, 82bl, 82t, 82br

Pictures of Britain: Norman Browne: 23t; Keith Ellis: 39br; Norman Feakins: 75t; Deryck Lister Hallam: 41t, 62b; Adam Swaine: 72–3; Adina Tovy: 66bl; Julian Worker: 18b

Rex Features: 46bl; Alexander Caminada: 33t; Mauro Carraro: 83br; James Fraser: 84t; Patrick Frilet: 78t, 78b; Richard Gardner: 32tr; David Hartley: 21t; JD/Keystone USA: 46b; LXO: 74t; Peter Macdiarmid: 18t; Dan Sparham: 80, 80br; The Travel Library: 61b, 61t; Joan Williams: 77b

Stowe House Preservation Trust/Jerry Hardman-Jones: 32tc, 32b

Joy Wotton: 3, 4ml, 4 mr, 88t, 89t, 90, 91, 92 t and b, 93, 10tc, 39bl

Peter Wotton: 1, 4bl, 5br, 10tl, 22br, 85br

Below: Balmoral, Victoria's 'dear paradise'.